D1309078

"*Stork Avenue is proud to be associated with* The Child Safety Guide for New and Expecting Parents. *We have helped many parents announce their babies during the past 10 years. We also want to help parents keep them safe. We believe this book will help all parents safely prepare for their baby's arrival and help keep them safe during their first years.*"

— *Bob Hunter*
Founder & President, Stork Avenue Inc.

What people are saying about
The Child Safety Guide for New and Expecting Pa___

"One of the most common reasons for pediatric emergency room visits is accidents at home. The great majority of these accidents are preventable. As a pediatrician, I try very hard to advise parents about how to make their homes a safe haven. Information and education are the most effective tools for parents and caretakers to keep children safe. The Child Safety Guide for New and Expecting Parents *provides very useful and important information in order to keep our children from harm."*

— Y. Aaron Kaweblum, MD
Pediatrician

"Parental awareness – it's key to preventing injuries among kids under age 5. I say this as a pediatrician with more than 22 years in practice. The Child Safety Guide for New and Expecting Parents *provides moms and dads with the information they need to keep their young children from harm at home or while out driving. It's a terrific resource and a welcome addition to the safe parenting literature."*

— Peggy Solomon-Bergen, MD
Pediatrician

"As a pediatrician and soon-to-be mom, I'm keenly aware of how important child safety is to protecting infants and toddlers. This convenient guide provides parents with the information they need to identify hazards and prevent injuries. It's a wonderfully handy book for anyone who has young children, or who's about to become a parent for the first time."

— Alissa Zenack, DO
Pediatrician

"A must-read for all caretakers of children!"

— Howard S. Gill, MD
Pediatrician

"I highly recommend The Child Safety Guide for New and Expecting Parents. *The book provides parents with a great foundation in child safety. I also think the large font, many illustrations and friendly layout make the book easy to read for the many sleep deprived parents who will read it."*

— Richard M. Handal, MD
Obstetrics & Gynecology

"In the ER I regularly encounter the consequences of inadequate attention to child safety. These injuries, so many of which could easily have been prevented, have an added impact on me as mother of a one-year-old. I think all parents of young children would benefit from this convenient, comprehensive guide."

— Elana Beckerman, MD
University of Chicago Hospitals

"The Child Safety Guide for New and Expecting Parents *is the most comprehensive book on child safety that I have ever read! The content is superbly organized and it is presented in an easily readable and pleasant format. Parents and children alike will be greatly served by this book.*"

— Miranda Brual, RN
CEO, Home Nurse Inc.

"Protecting our children is one of the most fundamental aspects in parenting. The Child Safety Guide for New and Expecting Parents *provides well organized content to empower parents to keep their children safe.*"

— William Scherer, DPM, MS

"As a leading website dedicated to new and expectant parents, Babiesonline.com only recommends quality products and services to our families. The Child Safety Guide for New and Expecting Parents *is one of those quality products! The book provides outstanding child safety content and presents it in a well organized and visually pleasing manner. It merits a place on the book shelf of every new and expectant parent.*"

— Shannon Anderson
Founder and President, Babiesonline.com

"There is nothing more important than keeping our children safe from harm. As a mother, grandmother, and founder of several preschools since 1979, I highly recommend this book to all expectant parents, parents and caregivers."

— Janice Barbarito
President, Barbarito and Beyers Preschools
NJ Mother of the Year, 2003

"Chris Bezick has accomplished in The Child Safety Guide for New and Expecting Parents *what I devote my life to, helping people help themselves. This book will give us the knowledge and the power to raise our children in a safe environment. This is a must read!*"

— O   Periu
National speaker, Best sellir   of
How to Raise Happy, Healthy and Su
Investigative Selling; and From Manageme

CHICAGO PUBLIC LIBRARY
R0302858305

The Child Safety Guide
for New and Expecting Parents

Christian J. Bezick

The Child Safety Guide for New and Expecting Parents can be purchased online at www.thechildsafetyguide.com or through Stork Avenue by calling 1-800-861-5437. Special discounts are available for bulk orders.

SafeKids Books

A Division of the American Family Safety Network
1500 South Dixie Highway, Third Floor
Coral Gables, FL 33146

Copyright © 2004 by Christian J. Bezick

All rights reserved, including the right of reproduction in whole or in part in any form. Requests for such permissions should be addressed to the publisher at the address provided above.

Cover design, book layout and illustrations by Andrea Flanders

Editor: Carl Flanders

Manufactured in the United States of America

Bezick, Christian J.
     The Child Safety Guide for New and Expecting Parents/
     Christian J. Bezick.

ISBN 0-9758895-0-8

Library of Congress Control Number: 2004094661

This publication contains the opinions and ideas of its author. It is not intended as a substitute for doctor's advice or any product manufacturer's labels, warnings or instructions. No warranty is made with respect to the accuracy or completeness of the information contained herein, and both the author and publisher specifically disclaim any responsibility for any liability, loss or risk, personal or otherwise, which is incurred as a consequence, directly or indirectly, of the use and application of any of the contents of this book.

To Owen and Oliver

Acknowledgements

I could never have undertaken, much less completed, a work of this scope without the generous help and support of others. To them, I am indebted.

I owe my own abiding interest in the subject of this book to my two sons. Owen introduced me to the joy of being a dad and inspired my initial interest in child safety. And Ollie, with his boundless energy and daredevil spirit, has challenged me on a daily basis to practice what I preach about safety.

To my wife, Lisa, a special thank you. Her encouragement and support from start to finish made this book possible.

I'd also like to thank the following individuals for their indispensable contributions:

Through their commitment to child safety and extraordinary talent, my editor, Carl Flanders, and graphic designer and illustrator, Andrea Flanders, took my draft work and made this book what it is.

Consumer safety expert Bill Kitzes, who regularly makes time to discuss child safety issues with me. I not only have the utmost respect for his extensive child safety knowledge, but also look to him as a parent role model. He and his wife have raised two wonderful children. I look forward to continuing our spirited discourse into the future.

Bob Hunter, founder and president of Stork Avenue, for wholeheartedly supporting this book, for lending his expertise to its development, and above all, for being such a stalwart friend throughout.

I also want to acknowledge the following federal government agencies as vital information sources for this book:

- The Consumer Product Safety Commission (CPSC)
- The National Highway Traffic Safety Administration (NHTSA)
- The Centers for Disease Control and Prevention (CDC)

These public organizations make an invaluable contribution to child safety in the United States and deserve to be recognized for it.

Finally, I'd like to salute my readers, for your interest in and commitment to child safety. I hope you learn a lot over the course of this book and are inspired to get other parents you know to increase their child safety awareness.

◢ TABLE OF CONTENTS ◣

CHAPTER

1

Introduction to Child Safety

Becoming a parent is a blessing beyond compare. Children make our lives rich and fulfilled in ways we can't fathom until they come along. Yes, they deprive us of sleep and tax our energy. They drive us nuts, now and then. And sometimes they worry us sick. But through it all, they are our greatest joy.

Our instinct to protect and nurture them starts before they show up, during pregnancy. When they arrive, our protective urge becomes even more powerful as we hold them in our arms and experience a love like no other. We can't imagine what life was like before them. And, whether it's feeding, bathing, or putting them to bed, we want to keep them safe. Always.

Our protective impulse as parents is a normal expression of our loving concern. What's more, we come to know all too soon that young children and safety hazards have an uncanny ability to find each other.

Protecting our children, vulnerable as they are in their first years, is not only our impulse – it's our basic responsibility. It requires us to take all reasonable steps to keep our infants and toddlers from crossing paths with dangers of whatever kind in their everyday environment. Before we can, of course, we must be able to recognize hazards in the first place.

This book, simply put, is devoted to helping you meet this responsibility. It aims to do so by providing you with the information and guidance you need to maintain your home as a fundamentally safe place for your child.

We'll get started with your practical introduction to child safety from birth to age 5 years in the next chapter. Before we do, we'll provide some context for our topic by outlining the scope of early childhood injuries, explaining why they happen, and describing the limits of parental instinct in keeping young children safe.

▷ THE INJURY TOLL ◁

According to the Consumer Product Safety Commission (CPSC), approximately 1.7 million children under the age of 5 were treated in hospital emergency rooms in 2002 for injuries from consumer products. And, for every 2 children treated in ERs, there were 3 treated for injuries in medical offices and clinics. Thus, more than 4 million children under age 5, or roughly 22% of this population segment, were injured and required medical attention in 2002. And keep in mind that these figures do *not* include injuries suffered in auto accidents. What these numbers reveal is that far too many children under age 5 get hurt each year.

WHY DO THESE INJURIES OCCUR?

On a percentage basis, children under age 5 are injured nearly 2 times more than the rest of the US population. We might expect other age groups to be at least as susceptible to injury. The elderly, for example, who are prone to falls or other accidents because of physical frailty. Or teens and young adults, who get hurt playing sports or doing the reckless things they're inclined to do.

So why do kids under age 5 get hurt almost twice as much as the rest of us? The answer lies in the very nature of this first phase of life. From birth to 5 is when kids are developing their motor skills and sensory perceptions and applying them in a world whose every feature is brand new to them. And, they're doing so with the very limited understanding and judgment about safety risks which children under 5 possess. This is a formula for mishaps and, by extension, injuries.

SAFETY MUST BE LEARNED

Before your baby arrived, the thought of becoming a parent may have had you anxious or even feeling overwhelmed. Such awesome responsibility – and yet no experience to guide you! Not long after you brought your child home from the hospital, though, you figured out how to care for him. And soon enough, you were an "old pro" at parenting basics. That's because a lot of what we must do as parents comes pretty naturally, given a little experience.

The protective impulse is perhaps our most basic instinct as parents. But it's important for us to recognize its limits. For example, we don't instinctively know all possible threats to our children's safety. Hazard recognition isn't "hard wired" in us. Neither is knowing how to minimize or altogether eliminate potential threats. The fact is that much about child safety must be learned.

▷ SAFETY STARTS AT HOME ◁

To understand what's involved in keeping your child safe requires a strong grasp of how he interacts with his environment. His main environment by far in his first years is, of course, his home. It stands to reason, therefore, that child safety begins at home, and involves virtually anything your little one is bound to encounter there. Many if not most household items – furnishings, appliances, fixtures, or even structural features like windows or doors – pose no threat to older kids or adults. But they may well be dangerous to children under age 5. In fact, more than half of all child injuries in 2002 were caused by items in the home. It's important to point out, too, that products made specifically for kids can also pose danger if they're either defective or used incorrectly.

▷ IT'S UP TO YOU ◁

Looking out for your child's safety, in and outside your home, falls squarely on you. So, where do you turn to learn about this vitally important subject? There is, after all, no local public child safety agency standing by, ready to train you. You're really on your own. To help you get your child safety bearings, we've developed this guide as your starting point. It's meant to provide a sound foundation in the basics of child safety – hazards, preventive measures, and corrective actions. These are the basics you need to master as a parent entrusted with keeping your child from harm.

We cover the following major topics in the span of 14 chapters:

+ Childproofing

+ Sleep safety

+ Infant products

+ Product recalls

+ Car seats

+ Common household hazards (choking, poison, water, and window)

Our guide also makes additional practical child safety information and resources available to you in a series of appendices.

GOOD NEWS

The good (and comforting) news about child safety is that if you're well informed on the subject, and faithfully put into practice what you learn, there's an excellent likelihood you'll keep your child from coming to harm.

Parenting is the most demanding – and rewarding – job you'll ever have. It's a 24/7 undertaking. And it all starts with the basic responsibility of protecting your child. Therefore, making yourself knowledgeable about child safety should be a top parenting priority. *The Child Safety Guide for New and Expecting Parents* can be a handy and indispensable beginning source for your child safety education.

We'll begin your introduction with an overview of childproofing.

CHAPTER

2

Childproofing

Installing a gate at the top of stairs. Discarding a poisonous house plant. Cushioning the corners of a coffee table. These are all examples of childproofing, which could be defined as the measures we take to protect young children from safety hazards in their everyday environment. That environment, by and large, is their home. And home is where the vast majority of accidents and resulting injuries involving children happen. For parents, therefore, childproofing is an issue in their households, first and foremost.

We might also define childproofing by what it is *not*. It is not a substitute for proper adult supervision. Nor is it foolproof and failsafe. Even thorough childproofing is no guarantee against an accident ever occurring. What you can expect childproofing to do is

1. reduce the risk of accidents happening;

2. limit their seriousness if they do happen;

3. prepare you to take proper action in an emergency; and

4. protect your home and the things in it from the damage a small child can do.

We cover various aspects of childproofing elsewhere throughout this book. Our aim in this chapter is to provide parents with a "big picture" introduction to childproofing. We will identify common home hazards for young children and outline the general approaches to neutralizing them as threats. We also will identify a range of safety devices recommended for any household with children under age 5 years. Finally, we will present professional childproofing versus "do it yourself" as options for safeguarding your home.

Parents must bear in mind that childproofing is dynamic; as such, it evolves as children grow. It is not "do it once and you're done." As your child develops, the childproofing requirements in your home will change. So you need to stay on top of this evolution, recognizing that the hazards which threaten your little one will shift as she goes from being an infant to a toddler and later to a preschooler. When these developmental shifts happen, you'll need to modify your childproofing efforts accordingly, to keep pace.

▶ GENERAL APPROACHES ◀

There are 3 basic approaches to childproofing. What determines the proper approach to any given hazard is the nature and seriousness of the hazard. Let's take a look at these 3 approaches.

Removing Hazards

The surest way to neutralize a household hazard is, of course, to remove it altogether. If it's not there, it can do no harm. But removal has its practical limits. You can't – and needn't – remove *everything* which might pose a danger. Focus on removing notably hazardous items that serve no useful purpose any longer – for example, toxic household cleaners or other chemical products that have been languishing in the garage or under the sink, unused for many months (if not years). Other candidates include expired medications and poisonous indoor plants. You also should consider removing furniture items that are nothing but big trouble with a young child around – a glass coffee table, for example, or a cabinet with low glass doors.

Placing Barriers

As we said, emptying your home of everything that could be hazardous to your child would be wildly impractical. Imagine – you'd have to remove, among other items, knives, glasses, bottles, medications, cosmetics, laundry and dishwasher detergents, china, computers, plastic wrap, etc., etc. But so extreme an approach is not necessary. Common sense and experience tell us that a compromise approach provides suitable protection while letting us actually live in our homes. The compromise is to place barriers between your infant or toddler and home hazards of various kinds. And this is, by far, the childproofing approach most favored by parents.

Barriers include any safety device that separates hazard from child – e.g., a latch, a lock, a gate, an outlet cover, a fence, a childproof cap, etc. For optimal safety, barriers should be installed in multiple layers, when warranted by the seriousness of the hazard.

Let's illustrate layering with the example of a laundry room where toxic substances are stored: There would be a door knob cover on the laundry room door (layer 1), a safety latch on the storage cabinet (layer 2), and childproof caps on the toxic items in the cabinet (layer 3).

A discussion of barriers is a good opportunity to bring up fireplaces, which merit special attention as a hazard because young children are so drawn to them. A hearth's sharp corners and hard surfaces can inflict serious injuries to infants or toddlers. Fireplace implements may pose danger, as well. And, of course, the embers of a smoldering fire are extremely hazardous. If you have a fireplace in your home, your best approach to sealing it against your child's efforts to reach it is to install a fireplace gate, which will create a safety zone around the fireplace and hearth.

Cushioning

The third approach to childproofing is to cushion the hazard. Cushioning involves placement of padding or a bumper on the sharp corners and hard surfaces that babies could hit their heads on when they fall, as they invariably will. Consider cushioning things like lower kitchen cabinets, bathtubs, hearths, and sharp-cornered furniture. Cushioning won't prevent accidental falls, of course, but it will reduce the seriousness of injuries when they happen.

RECOMMENDED CHILDPROOFING DEVICES

There is a range of safety devices available to help parents protect their children from common household hazards. The best devices, from a consumer standpoint, are ones that provide protection as advertised *and* are easy for parents to install and use. You should always follow the manufacturer's instructions for installing a device. If you have older children, teach them to always re-secure a device after they've unsecured it (e.g., closing a safety gate they opened or refastening a latch on a kitchen cabinet). And remember that devices are not failsafe and should not be relied upon as a substitute for proper adult supervision.

Child safety devices are widely available at baby equipment outlets, hardware stores, supermarkets, drug stores and department stores, and through mail order catalogues.

Safety Note

Expert Advice: Look Out for These

Professional childproofers warn parents to be alert to the following household hazards, which sometimes get overlooked:

+ Banister railings — Spindles (or bars) spaced wider than $3\frac{1}{2}$ inches apart pose a strangulation hazard to a young child, whose body could fit through them, resulting in entrapment by the head and neck. Parents should consider installing a temporary Plexiglas or mesh barrier across spindles spaced more than $3\frac{1}{2}$ inches apart.

+ Cleansers — In nearly every household with young children, toxic cleansers are stored under the kitchen sink. Parents should either install a lock on the cabinet beneath the sink or move the cleansers to a cabinet well above ground level, out of children's reach.

+ Electrical outlets — An open outlet is an electrocution hazard. Parents should consider replacing existing outlet covers with safety plates that automatically cover the outlet when no plug is in it.

+ Salt — Table salt can be deadly if ingested by a baby. A tablespoon and a half of salt can be fatal to a child who weighs 25 pounds or less. Never leave salt out where a young child could reach it.

The professionals also advise parents to post emergency assistance numbers by every phone in their home.

The Consumer Product Safety Commission (CPSC) recommends the following safety devices for any household with children under 5 years of age:

1. **Safety latches and locks** to prevent access to cabinets or drawers where possible hazards (e.g., kitchen knives, medications, household cleaners) are kept. Latches and locks should be durable enough to withstand the pulling of a determined child yet convenient to install and easy to use. *Typical cost: under $2*

2. **Safety gates** to block access to stairs and other hazardous areas where an infant or toddler could come to harm. Gates that meet the latest safety standards have the Juvenile Products Manufacturers Association (JPMA) certification seal. (See Chapter 5 for more information on safety gates.) *Typical cost: $13 to $40*

3. **Door knob covers and door locks** to prevent young children from gaining access to rooms or areas with hazards. Covers thwart infants or toddlers by making it impossible for them to turn door knobs. A cover should be durable enough that it won't break with repeated use; but it must also be easy for an adult to manipulate so the door can be opened quickly in an emergency. *Typical cost of a door knob cover and door lock: $1; and $5 and up*

4. **Anti-scald devices** to prevent burns from hot water. These devices, which are installed on faucets and shower heads, regulate water temperature. In addition to utilizing these, parents should set the water heater temperature in their home at 120° Fahrenheit, maximum, to prevent accidental scalding. *Typical cost: $6 to $30*

5. **Smoke detectors** for early detection and warning of household fires. Install these essential safety devices on every level of your home and near all bedrooms so you and your family will be alerted in the event of a fire and can evacuate. You should check smoke alarms monthly to make sure they're working properly. *Typical cost: under $10*

6. **Window guards** to prevent falls from windows. The space between window guard bars should not exceed 4 inches. Any wider and a small child could fit through them. (See Chapter 13 for further information on window guards.) *Typical cost: $8 to $16*

7. **Safety netting** to prevent falls from balconies, decks, and landings. Check netting often to ensure it's properly installed and for signs of wear. *Typical cost: $8 to $16*

8. **Corner/edge bumpers** to prevent injuries (especially head injuries) from falls against sharp corners or edges of furniture or fireplaces. These bumpers affix to the sharp corners/edges and provide a protective cushion. *Typical cost: $1 and up*

9. **Outlet covers and outlet plates** to prevent electrical shock by blocking access to open wall outlets. Covers are the small plastic pronged devices that plug into the outlets. Plates are installed over the outlet and affixed with a screw to the outlet fixture. *Typical cost: under $2*

10. **Carbon monoxide (CO) detector** for early detection and warning of CO build up, which can be fatal. Carbon monoxide is a colorless, odorless gas that's very deadly when concentrated. Households with oil or gas heating systems or attached garages need these devices, which should be installed near all sleeping areas. *Typical cost: $30 to $70*

11. **Window cord safety tassels** to prevent the strangulation risk posed by loops in window blind cords. The tassel is affixed to the cord after the cord loop is cut. (See Chapter 13 for additional information on cord safety tassels.)

Safety tassels are available for free from the Window Covering Safety Council. Order by calling (800) 506-4636.

12. **Door stops and door holders** to prevent injuries to hands and fingers. These stops and holders help keep small hands and fingers from getting pinched or crushed in doors and door hinges. *Typical cost: under $4*

13. **Cordless phone** to enable parents to answer the phone without any break in visual supervision of young children. A cordless phone is especially handy for parents when little ones are in or near water at home and require continuous supervision. *Typical cost: $30 and up*

WHO'S DOING THE CHILDPROOFING?

Childproofing takes time and labor – and more than a little handiness. Who's going to undertake this effort in your home? Here are your options: hire a professional; or do it yourself. Let's have a word about each, in turn.

Professional Childproofers

Society's greater awareness of and attentiveness to child safety has spawned a new member of the service economy: the professional childproofer. Hiring a pro can offer parents the following advantages:

+ An experienced childproofer really knows the ropes. He or she can quickly identify hazards that new parents wouldn't even recognize as potential dangers, for their lack of experience.

+ A professional knows what safety device or equipment works best in a given situation, with a particular hazard. He or she can draw on experience to select the optimal device for providing protection.

+ Professionals are aware of and have access to the best safety devices. Where parents might find only a single type or brand of safety product at a retail outlet, a professional can go through wholesalers for a broad range of products.

+ A pro works fast. It might take parents a month's worth of weekends to finish childproofing, where a skilled professional could complete the job in a fraction of that time.

If you do consider going this route, you'll want to find someone who is verifiably qualified. Don't be shy about asking whomever you might hire to furnish proof of his or her credentials. And it's always a smart idea to ask for customer/client references – i.e., other parents for whom the professional has done work.

Do It Yourself

If you choose to undertake childproofing yourself, you'll be like the vast majority of parents, for whom staying a step ahead of household hazards becomes a rite of parenthood. You'll need a decent set of tools. And it helps to have a high frustration threshold. But keep in mind the reward – by childproofing your home, you'll make it somewhere your curious and fast developing baby can roam and explore without fear (*your* fear) that she'll come to harm.

Your starting point should be to draw up a comprehensive childproofing plan for your home. The plan should identify all hazards and where they're located; specify what steps you need to take to childproof the hazards; and identify the safety devices required to complete the childproofing.

One approach you might take is to draw up a blueprint of your home. You can do this simply by sketching a floor plan, including each room, on a piece of paper. If you have multiple floors, use separate sheets of paper for each floor. Once you have your floor plan, you can start by marking off any rooms or areas that need to be strictly "off limits" to your baby; and next to them, specify how you'll restrict access (e.g., install a safety gate or door knob cover).

Then, for each remaining room or area, begin identifying and inventorying potential hazards. Take your child's bedroom, for example. You might list 6 electrical outlets, 4 windows, 1 radiator, 3 drawers, and 2 curtain cords. Beside each identified hazard you would then list how (i.e., with what devices) you intend to childproof it – e.g., by installing 6 outlet safety plates, 3 window guards and 1 window stop, a safety gate, 3 drawer latches, and 2 cord safety tassels. When you finish your blueprint, you'll have your complete plan-of-action checklist, which can double as your safety device shopping list.

How do you know all the hazards to look for around your home? Educate yourself. Start by consulting child safety information sources such as this book for guidance. And solicit the knowledge of family members and friends with young children who've already been through the childproofing process. Beyond these steps, there's another one that might prove very helpful in identifying hazards: View your home from your child's perspective – literally. In each room, get down on the floor, at your baby's level, and have a look around. See and experience the room from the same vantage point that she does. You'll be surprised how you're able to see dangers or trouble areas that weren't visible to you before you took a knee or lay down.

REVIEW OF KEY SAFETY POINTS

Let's summarize the key points covered in this chapter:

✔ Childproofing covers all the measures we take to protect young children from safety hazards in their everyday environment.

✔ Childproofing is no substitute for proper adult supervision.

✔ Childproofing is dynamic – as your child grows, you need to modify your childproofing efforts to keep pace.

✔ 3 general approaches to childproofing:

1. Removing hazards

2. Placing barriers

3. Cushioning

✔ The CPSC recommends the following safety devices for households with children under age 5:

- Safety latches and locks

- Safety gates

- Door knob covers and door locks

- Anti-scald devices

- Smoke detectors

- Window guards

- Safety netting

- Corner/edge bumpers

- Electrical outlet covers and plates

- Carbon monoxide detectors

- Window cord safety tassels

- Door stops and door holders

- Cordless phone

Professional Childproofers

✔ Advantages with professional childproofer:

- Experience (knows the childproofing ropes)

- Expert knowledge of safety devices/equipment

- Access to best safety products

- Works fast

✔ Professionals warn parents to be alert to the following hazards:

- Banister railings (entrapment hazard)

- Toxic cleaners (poison hazard)

- Electrical outlets (electrical shock hazard)

- Salt (can be fatal if swallowed by a baby)

Do It Yourself

✔ 3-step planning for childproofing your home:

1. Identify all hazards

2. Specify childproofing steps

3. Identify safety devices needed to complete childproofing

✔ Solicit childproofing pointers from family members and friends with young children.

✔ Viewing your home literally from your child's perspective (i.e., get down on all fours) may help you identify hazards.

This completes our overview of childproofing. In the coming 2 chapters, we turn our attention to sleep time safety, starting with cribs and bassinets.

CHAPTER
3

The Safe Crib

You just found out you're pregnant! Soon enough, you'll be busy planning how to set up the nursery. You'll have lots of decisions to make about what baby furniture to get. For your newborn's safety, no decision is more important than choosing a suitable crib. Sleep safety begins with crib safety.

Your baby will sleep upwards of 12 hours a day through infancy and into early toddlerhood. That's a lot of crib time. And much of it will be spent outside your watchful eye. Yes, you'll check in on him now and then. But you can't watch him constantly when he's sleeping – not if you ever hope to get some sleep yourself! So knowing he's in a safe crib is crucial to your peace of mind.

The fact is that crib injuries, when they happen, tend to be serious – even life-threatening. Many parents just assume that crib death is always a case of Sudden Infant Death Syndrome (SIDS). But this isn't so. Tragedy also can strike during sleep time for reasons other than SIDS.

The 2 keys to sleep safety for your new baby are 1) make sure his crib is safe; and 2) make certain he sleeps in an overall safe and hazard-free environment. Our aim in this chapter is to help parents select a safe crib and then maintain it for safe use. We also cover important safety considerations with bassinets and cradles, which many parents choose as their newborn's initial sleep habitat. In Chapter 4, we cover other important factors that impact sleep safety.

▶ SELECTING A CRIB ◀

The first decision you'll face is whether to buy new or used. A brand new crib is the safer way to go because it will meet all current safety standards. A used crib, on the other hand, might not. The older the crib, the less likely it is to conform to today's safety standards.

Suppose you decide to get a used crib at a consignment shop. Or say you chose to re-use one you already own – i.e., a crib an older child of yours once slept in. In either case, you need to evaluate whether it's still safe to use. The Consumer Product Safety Commission (CPSC) has provided the following crib safety checks to guide your evaluation.

Crib Checks

A general warning is in order before we get to specifics: If a crib fails to meet *any* of the following CPSC safety guidelines, it's unsafe for your child – or for any child – and must not be used.

Crib slats
Crib slats are the vertical bars that prevent a baby from falling out or (eventually) a toddler from climbing out.

A safe crib has slats that are spaced no more than $2\,3/8$ inches apart. Any wider, and an infant's body could squeeze through them; and if it did, the baby's head could get trapped against the slats, creating a strangulation risk. The simplest way to check crib slat spacing is the "soda can test." Try to pass a soda can through the slats. If the can fits through them, the slat spacing is too wide.

Safety keys:

+ The space between crib slats should be no more than 2 3/8 inches (about the diameter of a soda can).

+ A crib with loose or missing slats is unsafe for use.

Crib mattress

The safest crib mattress fits snugly in the crib frame. Use the "2-finger test" to check the fit. The space between the mattress and crib should be no more than 2 fingers wide. Any wider, and an infant's head could get trapped in the space. And if so trapped, a baby could suffocate.

Safety keys:

+ Use only a tight-fitting crib mattress.

+ Plastic wrapping is a suffocation hazard. Remove any such wrapping from the mattress before ever letting your baby sleep on it.

+ Never use a plastic bag as a mattress cover. It, too, is a suffocation hazard to infants.

Crib sheets

Safety requires that a crib sheet fit snugly on the mattress. A loose fitting sheet, or one that pulls free of the mattress too easily, is unsafe because a sleeping baby can become entangled in it. And a baby whose face gets covered by a loose sheet could suffocate.

Safety keys:

+ Make sure the crib sheet fits the mattress snugly. How snugly? The sheet shouldn't come off the mattress when you pull any corner of it.

+ Never use an adult bed sheet on a crib mattress. It can too easily come loose and pose a suffocation hazard to a sleeping baby.

Corner posts

A corner post is a post, finial, or decorative knob located at the crib's top corners, where the side panels meet the headboard and footboard. You won't find these posts on new cribs because they don't meet today's safety standards. But they're fairly common on older cribs. And they can be a real hazard. Such posts become dangerous catch points for clothing once an infant is able to pull himself to a standing position in the crib. Pajamas or a "onesie" that snag on a catch point can put a baby at risk of strangulation.

A crib corner post should not extend more than $1/16$ of an inch. Any taller, and it should be sawed flush with the headboard or footboard. Also, decorative knobs on corner posts should be removed. When removing posts or knobs, be sure to sand down any splinters or sharp corners.

Safety keys:

+ Crib corner posts should be less than $1/16$ of an inch high. (The only exception to this rule is if the posts are over 16 inches tall, as on a canopy-style crib.)

+ A crib with decorative knobs, finials, or corner posts is unsafe for use.

Mattress support hangers/screws

The crib mattress is supported by mattress support hangers or screws. If one of these unhooks or falls out, a space can form between the mattress and either the headboard, footboard, or side rail. Any such space is dangerous to a sleeping baby, who could get trapped in it and be strangled.

The entrapment risk is even greater if the mattress happens to slope toward the corner. Why? Because a baby would be more prone to slide down the slope toward a space created by an unfastened mattress support.

Safety keys:

+ All mattress support hangers should be secured with bolts, screws, or closed hooks.

+ Check all mattress supports after a crib is moved or assembled to make sure they are secure.

Hardware

Loose or missing hardware is a big deal in terms of safety. A crib with loose or missing hardware could easily collapse. It's also more prone to dangerous spaces forming between the mattress and crib frame.

Safety keys:

+ Make sure your baby's crib has all its hardware – and that it's all fastened tight – before you put him in it.

+ Never place your baby in a crib with missing or broken hardware.

Headboard & footboard

Some older cribs may have cut-out designs on the headboard or footboard. These openings can be dangerous if a baby's head is able to fit through them. If a decorative cut-out is wide enough, it's a strangulation hazard. Your safest bet is to altogether avoid a crib with cut-out designs on the head- or footboard.

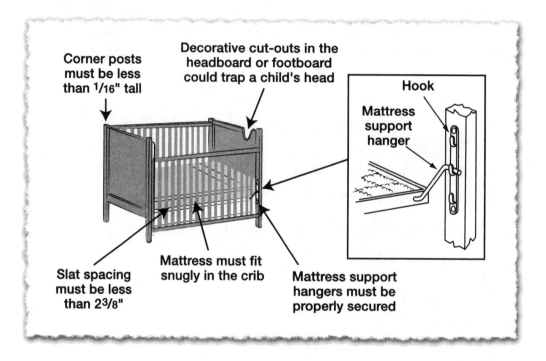

Corner posts must be less than 1/16" tall

Decorative cut-outs in the headboard or footboard could trap a child's head

Hook

Mattress support hanger

Slat spacing must be less than 2³/₈"

Mattress must fit snugly in the crib

Mattress support hangers must be properly secured

BASSINETS

Let's back track, so to speak, and take a look at bassinets. A lot of parents initially elect to put their newborn in a bassinet (or cradle) rather than a crib. The bassinet doesn't replace a crib; rather it's an alternative sleep place for a baby in the first months of infancy.

A bassinet offers a couple of key advantages. First, being smaller than a crib, it tends to be comforting to a newborn, who feels more secure in its cozier space. Second, it's portable, which, beyond all else, is a welcome convenience for a nursing mom. (A chronically sleep deprived mom, we should add!) A bassinet is easy to move around a room or between rooms. At night, you could put it within arm's reach of your bed so you're able to quickly retrieve your hungry little one when that 2 am feeding rolls around. Then during the day you could roll it from your bedroom to another room, if you care to have your napping baby closer by. Most models fit through a standard door fully assembled.

But bassinets can be hazardous if they're designed poorly or used improperly. According to the CPSC, hundreds of babies get treated in hospital ERs every year for injuries suffered in bassinet or cradle accidents. Experience tells us that the main dangers associated with these mini-cribs are the following:

+ Collapsing   + Tipping over   + Entrapment

If you plan to have your baby sleep in a bassinet in his first months, you need to be alert to these 3 potential hazards.

Selecting a Bassinet

For optimal safety, a bassinet should have certain features. Here's what you should look for:

+ A wide, sturdy base for stability (i.e., less likely to tip over).

+ Strong, stable legs to prevent tipping over.

+ A bassinet with folding legs should have a mechanism that locks the legs in the upright position when the bassinet is in use. Accidental collapse of folding legs is a leading cause of injuries with bassinets.

+ A firm, smooth mattress to help prevent accidental suffocation and SIDS.

+ A snug-fitting mattress to prevent entrapment. It should fit flush inside the frame. A newborn can get wedged even in a narrow space between the mattress and frame. If so, his face can become trapped against the bassinet's side, putting him at risk of suffocation. The space should be no wider than your 2 fingers – index and middle – held together.

+ Some bassinet models have spindles or slats. As with cribs, the width between them should be no more than 2 3/8 inches.

+ No rough or sharp edges on the interior of the frame. Be alert to this issue especially with a wicker or woven bassinet.

+ A bassinet with wheels should have a brake mechanism that immobilizes them so the bassinet cannot move with a baby in it.

Also, if you prefer a bassinet with a hood, look for one with a folding hood. A hood that doesn't fold back can become a nuisance when you go to lay down or pick up your baby.

Safe-Use Guidelines

Once you have a bassinet that meets suggested safety standards, you then need to be sure to use it properly. Adhering to the following guidelines will help ensure that your newborn's bassinet experience is always safe:

+ Does your bassinet have a stand with folding legs? If so, when setting it up, make sure the legs are extended to the full open position and locked in place.

+ Always put your baby to sleep on his back in the bassinet, to reduce the risk of accidental suffocation and SIDS. (See Chapter 4 for further information on sleep positioning.)

+ Always lock the wheels in place when your baby is in the bassinet.

+ Don't permit older siblings or pets near the bassinet when your baby is in it. In an unsupervised moment, they could tip or knock it over.

+ Never move the bassinet from one location to another with your baby in it. Doing so puts him at risk of injury if the bassinet collapsed or tipped over.

You should also take the following precautions regarding the mattress and bedding:

+ Use only the original mattress from the manufacturer.

+ Never place a towel or other extra padding on the mattress because it poses a suffocation hazard and raises the SIDS risk.

+ Don't put any soft bedding (e.g., pillow, comforter, or quilt) or stuffed animals in the bassinet with your baby because they pose a suffocation hazard.

For safety's sake, you need to know when it's time to switch your baby from bassinet to crib. A bassinet has recommended height and weight maximums. These are the height and weight beyond which an infant can't safely remain in the bassinet. Know these limits for your bassinet. You're wisest to make the switch to a crib before your baby reaches the height and weight maximums. But in any case, a bassinet generally isn't designed to hold a baby beyond 3 or 4 months of age. Infants simply outgrow them.

CRADLES

A cradle, essentially, is a bassinet that rocks, back and forth, on a rocker. There are 2 types of cradles: rocking (mounted on a rocker) and swinging (mounted on a swing). Both offer the same functional feature – gentle, rhythmic motion to settle an infant and lull him to sleep. In terms of safety, bassinets and cradles have the same basic profile: What's true for bassinets – injury risks, safety standards, and use guidelines – is true for cradles, as well.

But cradles do pose a special hazard: A cradle can rock too far in one direction or the other if its locking pins aren't working properly. In such case, the steep angle of the rocking could force a baby to roll clear to one side, flush against the cradle wall. The baby's full weight on the one side then could prevent the cradle from rocking back in the other direction. The cradle would be stuck in that position, with the baby pressed against the side, unable to free himself, and therefore at risk of suffocation from the pressure of the cradle wall against his chest. You can avoid this hazard by taking a couple of precautions: First, make sure the cradle cannot rock more than 5 degrees in either direction. And second, regularly inspect the locking pins, which prevent the cradle from rocking too far, left or right; make sure they're undamaged and securely in place.

REVIEW OF KEY SAFETY POINTS

Let's summarize the key points covered in this chapter:

Cribs

- ✔ New cribs must meet all current safety standards; used cribs might not.

- ✔ The spacing between crib slats should be no wider than 2 3/8 inches.

- ✔ A crib with loose or missing slats is unsafe for use.

- ✔ The space between the mattress and crib frame should be no more than 2 fingers wide.

- ✔ Remove any plastic wrapping from the crib mattress before letting your baby sleep on it.

- ✔ Never use an adult bed sheet on a crib mattress.

- ✔ Make sure the crib sheet fits the mattress snugly.

- ✔ Crib corner posts should be less than 1/16 inch high.

- ✔ Mattress support hangers should be secured with bolts, screws, or closed hooks.

- ✔ Never place your baby in a crib with hardware missing or broken hardware.

Bassinets

- ✔ 3 main dangers associated with bassinets:

  - Collapsing

  - Tipping over

  - Entrapment

- ✔ Recommended safety features:

  - Wide, sturdy base

  - Strong, stable legs

  - Locking mechanism on folding legs

  - Firm, smooth mattress

  - Snug-fitting mattress

  - Folding hood (on any model with a hood)

  - Brake mechanism on any model with wheels

- ✔ Always place your baby to sleep on his back in the bassinet.

- ✔ Always lock the wheels in place when your baby's in the bassinet.

- ✔ Don't permit older siblings or pets near the bassinet when your baby is in it.

- ✔ Never place a towel or other extra padding on the crib mattress.

- ✔ Don't put any soft bedding in the bassinet with your baby.

✔ Switch your baby to a crib before he reaches the bassinet's height and weight limits.

Cradles

✔ Be alert to the special hazard posed by a cradle if its locking pins aren't working properly.

✔ Inspect locking pins regularly for damage or displacement.

✔ Make sure your baby's cradle can't rock more than 5 degrees in either direction.

In our next chapter, we move beyond cribs and bassinets to cover the other important considerations in sleep safety.

CHAPTER
4

Placing Your Baby to Sleep

Your baby sleeps a lot. (If you're lucky, that is!) What's most important, of course, is to make sure she sleeps safely. As a parent, you could be putting your child at risk of harm during sleep time and not even realize it. Which is why it's so important for you to learn the basics of sleep safety.

Let's start your education with this chapter. In considering sleep safety, we'll cover the following topics:

- ✦ Crib set-up

- ✦ Sleepwear

- ✦ Sleep position

- ✦ Adult beds

- ✦ Crib adjustments as your child grows

- ✦ The crib-to-bed transition

- ✦ Toddler beds and bunk beds

Adhering to sleep safety "dos and don'ts" will put your mind at ease whenever you put your baby down for slumber.

SETTING UP THE CRIB

You've acquired a crib that meets current safety standards. You've assembled it according to the manufacturer's instructions. And you've covered the mattress with a tight-fitting bottom crib sheet. You're all set up, right? Not so fast. There are a few other things you need to do to be sure the crib is a perfectly safe place in which to put your little one.

Placement

You want to position the crib in the nursery so that it's well clear of some common dangers. For example, it should be far enough from window blind or curtain cords that a tiny hand couldn't reach through the slats and grab them. Such cords are a strangulation hazard for infants and tots. Also, the crib shouldn't be against the wall, directly beneath hanging picture frames or other hard objects.

Be careful not to hang items such as a diaper bag or toys on the crib frame because these, too, can pose a strangulation risk. It's OK, however, to mount a mobile (or crib gym) on the crib so long as it's beyond your baby's reach. Mobiles can be delightful entertainment for infants. But once your baby is pushing up on her hands and knees in the crib, it's time to remove the mobile.

Bedding

When we grow up, we like our bedding soft and billowy because it's most comfortable. But for babies, "soft and fluffy" is unsafe when it comes to bedding. Soft and fluffy pillows, comforters, cushions, sheepskins, and blankets pose a suffocation hazard to a sleeping infant. Indeed, a study by the Consumer Product Safety Commission (CPSC) found that babies put to sleep on soft bedding are at much greater risk of suffocation. Given this risk, you're wisest to keep your baby's crib free of any soft bedding. This means no stuffed animals or fluffy toys in the crib, either.

Dressing your baby in a sleeper is safer than tucking her in with a blanket. If you do choose to use a blanket, take the following precautions:

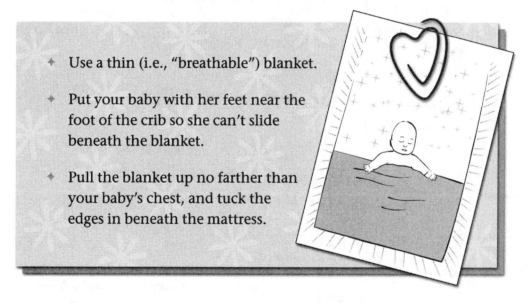

+ Use a thin (i.e., "breathable") blanket.

+ Put your baby with her feet near the foot of the crib so she can't slide beneath the blanket.

+ Pull the blanket up no farther than your baby's chest, and tuck the edges in beneath the mattress.

Bumpers

It's safe to outfit your baby's crib with bumpers, so long as they 1) fit around the entire crib (no space between pads); 2) tie or snap into place; and 3) have ties/snaps in each corner, on the top and bottom edges, and in the middle of each of the crib's long sides. Make sure you trim any slack from the ties to remove this possible strangulation hazard. And you should remove the bumpers once your baby is able to stand up in the crib so she can't use them to help her climb out.

Safety Note

Pacifiers, Strings, Cords & Necklaces

Every year, the CPSC reports several deaths of children under age 2 who are strangled by strings, cords, ribbons, or necklaces. Most of these involve infants who get pacifiers tethered to a string wrapped around their necks. In other cases, the children are wearing necklaces. These tragic accidents often happen in a crib or playpen, when the item around the child's neck catches on the furniture and entraps her.

To prevent such a mishap in your home, take the following precautions:

+ In general, never tie anything with a string (e.g., a pacifier or toy), or which is itself like a string (e.g., a necklace), around your infant's neck.

+ Never put your baby to bed with a pacifier tethered to a string around her neck.

+ Remove a bib or other clothing fastened around your baby's neck before putting her in a crib or playpen.

▶ SLEEPWEAR ◀

With baby sleepwear, the safest fit is a snug fit. Loose-fitting pajamas are a safety no-no, for 2 reasons. First, a loose-fitting garment could snag on the crib when the sleeping baby moves around, putting her in danger of getting trapped. And second, loose-fitting clothes – especially if they're cotton or cotton blend – ignite easily if exposed to fire and burn quickly because the air between the fabric and the child's skin feeds the flame. Snug-fitting clothes don't let much air between the fabric and the skin. Therefore, they're far less likely to catch on fire and they're not as flammable.

Flame Resistant Sleepwear

Fabric and fit are important safety considerations for children's sleepwear. Sleepwear should be flame resistant or snug-fitting to meet the US Consumer Product Safety Commission sleepwear requirements.

This garment is made of flame resistant fabric.

When you shop for your baby's sleepwear, always read the manufacturer's hangtag to make sure an item meets government safety standards for flammability and fire protection. Not all children's sleep clothing is flame resistant, unfortunately. When it's not, it should have a label alerting parents to this fact and reminding them that sleepwear should fit snugly.

For child's safety, garment should fit snugly. This garment is not flame resistant. Loose-fitting garment is more likely to catch fire.

It's a good idea to dress your baby in snug-fitting, flame-retardant sleepwear right from early infancy. But it's essential to do so once she can crawl – usually at 9 months or so – and is mobile enough to come in contact with stoves, fireplaces, furnaces, ash trays, and other fire sources.

SLEEP POSITION: BACK TO SLEEP

Which sleep position is safer for your baby: on her tummy (i.e., *prone*) or on her back (i.e., *supine*)? The answer is beyond debate: the safest sleep position for infants, by far, is on their back. A baby put to bed on her back is much less likely to accidentally suffocate or become a victim of Sudden Infant Death Syndrome (SIDS). What's more, research shows that sleeping on the stomach is a major risk factor for SIDS.

The CPSC and the American Academy of Pediatrics (AAP) both advise putting your baby to sleep on her back until age 1 to cut the risk of SIDS. Ten years ago, a nationwide "Back to Sleep" campaign was launched to educate parents about the great safety benefit of putting babies to sleep on their back. Since then, both prone sleeping and SIDS cases have declined dramatically. So the campaign has been a major plus for infant safety.

"Back to Sleep" – keep this simple safety slogan in mind when it's nap- or bedtime for your baby.

Who's Putting Your Baby to Bed?

For the first time since your baby arrived, you and your spouse are actually planning a night out together. Imagine – a date! Just the 2 of you. Just like old times. You've even lined up a babysitter – someone trustworthy from the neighborhood who has her own grown children, and who's more than happy to watch your newborn while you take a break.

Before you and your spouse step out, make sure your neighbor knows to put your baby to sleep on her back. Don't assume she does. Back when her kids were infants, she may have put them to bed on their tummy, as was then customary – and endorsed by pediatricians. (The clear link between prone sleep position and SIDS finally led the AAP to shift its recommendation on sleep position in 1992, when it began advising parents to put infants to sleep on their back.) So she might not even be aware that the supine sleeping position is now well established as safest for infants.

Don't be shy on this point. Make sure anyone who might look after your baby – whether it's daycare providers, babysitters, or grandparents – knows to put her to sleep on her back and understands the "Back to Sleep" message.

▷ ADULT BEDS ◁

If you're like most parents, you'll be tempted to bring your baby into bed with you from time to time. It might be to comfort her when she's crying. Or to comfort *you* when she's crying. Or just to snuggle. Whatever your reason, you really shouldn't share your bed with your baby. Doing so is unsafe and strongly discouraged by most pediatricians and child safety experts.

An infant sleeping in a grown-up bed could suffocate if an exhausted parent accidentally rolled over on her. Or a baby might get entangled in soft bedding, such as a pillow or thick comforter, and suffocate. An infant in an adult bed also is at risk of getting trapped, should she roll between the bed and a wall or between the mattress and bed frame.

For safety's sake, avoid the temptation to bring your baby into bed with you. A crib is the only reliably safe place for an infant to sleep.

▷ CRIB ADJUSTMENTS AS YOUR CHILD GROWS ◁

Your baby will grow fast. Before you know it, the tiny newborn you brought home from the hospital won't be so tiny any more. Throughout her first year (and beyond), you'll need to make adjustments to her crib so it remains a safe place for her to sleep as she gets bigger, stronger, more coordinated, and more mobile.

Let's outline these age-driven adjustments, from the time your baby first uses the crib until she's ready to make the move to a bed.

Starting Out

Your newborn's crib, of course, should meet current safety standards (see Chapter 3). And you'll want to follow all the safety precautions described previously under "Setting Up the Crib" in preparing the crib for your baby. For the first few months, you can keep the mattress at its highest setting because your little angel is no threat to go anywhere – not yet, at least.

When Your Baby Sits Up

Once your baby can sit up, she's at risk of falling out of her crib with the mattress at its highest setting. You can no longer rely on the crib sides to keep her from falling out. Therefore, when she turns 5 months old or begins to pull up on her hands and knees – whichever happens first – you should lower the mattress to the middle setting. This is also the right time to remove any mobiles or crib gyms from the crib because they pose a strangulation hazard to a child now strong and mobile enough to reach them.

When Your Baby Stands Up

By around her ninth month, your determined baby should be able to pull herself up to a standing position in the crib. Uh oh! Once she can hoist herself up, she's at risk of falling over the side of the crib. So it's time for you to adjust the mattress to its lowest setting, to prevent your baby from tumbling over the side and getting hurt. It's also time to remove any crib bumper pads because your clever infant might use them as a foothold to climb out.

Ready for the Crib-to-Bed Switch

When your child is either 35 inches tall or can scale the side of the crib, it's time to switch her to a bed. She should reach this milestone marker around 2 years of age.

▷ IT'S BED TIME ◁

Once your child outgrows the crib, you'll have to choose what kind of bed to move her to. Let's consider 2 of your options – toddler beds and bunk beds – and how each stacks up in terms of safety.

Toddler Beds

A toddler bed is the ideal transitional step from crib to big bed. A toddler (or youth) bed is smaller and lower to the ground than a full-size bed. Conveniently, it fits a standard-size crib mattress, so there's no need to buy another mattress. And most models feature a built-in guardrail to prevent a child from falling out while sleeping.

With toddler beds, there are a few safety points to note:

+ The distance from mattress to floor should be no more than 2 feet. Lower makes it easier for a child to climb in and out of bed. It also means a shorter fall in case the child accidentally rolls out of bed.

+ Look for a bed without corner post extensions (potential catch points) or decorative cut-outs in the headboard or footboard (possible entrapment hazard).

+ A built-in guardrail should be designed to prevent entrapment. There should be no sizable gap between rail and mattress in which a tot could get wedged. And be wary of a guardrail with loose mesh safety netting. Such netting bunches up, forming gaps through which a head or limb can slip and get tangled.

What's more, parents need to take precautions with where they place a toddler bed. It should be far enough from any windows that a child can't reach them from the bed. By extension, it should be beyond the reach of window blind or drapery cords, which pose a strangulation hazard to tots. And it shouldn't be situated beneath hanging picture frames or other hard objects mounted on a wall.

What can make toddler beds a favorite of kids is that they're available in many fun themes and designs, such as race cars, trains, fire trucks, princesses, and flowers.

Bunk Beds

You might fondly recall bunk beds from your own childhood. They're a convenient option for families that have – or plan to have – 2 kids close in age. The safety record for bunk beds, however, isn't so great. Every year, thousands of children under age 15 are treated in hospital ERs for injuries linked to bunk beds. Most of these injuries are fairly minor and result from accidental falls. And it's hardly surprising that these accidents often result from horseplay.

But there are some more serious potential safety hazards with bunk beds. Deadly hazards, even. These relate to children becoming trapped, in one way or another, and either suffocating or getting strangled as a result. Let's go over these hazards. Then we'll provide some important safety guidelines for selecting and using bunk beds.

Bunk bed hazards

With bunk beds, there are a number of key hazards you should be alert to:

1. **Guardrail spacing** – On some beds, the space between the guardrail and mattress, or between the bed frame and mattress, is wide enough

to allow a young child to slip through it. A child who falls through such a space can become suspended by her head and potentially strangle. Keep the following guideline in mind: The gap between the bed frame and the bottom of guard rails should be no more than 3¹/2 inches, to prevent entrapment.

On other beds, detachable guardrails can get dislodged if hardware comes loose. These guardrails are attached to the frame with hardware brackets, which can loosen over time due to body pressure against them. When this happens, the space between guardrail and frame widens to a point where it becomes a hazard. Thus, a sleeping child could get trapped in this space; or might fall out of bed because the rail is "derailed." Be on the lookout for this potential problem.

2. Beds without guardrails on both sides – Most bunk beds sold have a guardrail only on one side of the upper bunk to prevent falls. This design assumes that parents will locate the bed against a wall – and that the wall will act as the guardrail on that side. The problem is that a young child can roll off the mattress and get wedged between the bed and the wall, with dire results. You should never let your child on the upper bunk of bunk beds unless it has guardrails on both sides.

3. Dislodged mattress foundation – On some bunk beds, the mattress foundation rests on small ledges attached to the bed frame. These narrow support ledges can get dislodged, especially if someone on the bottom bunk pushes or kicks up on the top mattress. If the ledges do dislodge, the mattress and foundation will fall on the child in the bottom bunk. And children trapped under a collapsing mattress have suffocated.

Do you own a bunk bed with side rail ledges for mattress support? If so, you should add a cross-wire support beneath the top mattress. You can get a cross-wire support kit for free by writing to: Bunk Bed Kit, PO Box 2436, High Point, NC 27261.

4. Wrong size mattress – Bunk bed frames and mattresses come in 2 lengths: regular and extra long. Sometimes parents mistakenly buy a regular mattress for an extra-long bed. The result? A 5-inch gap between the mattress and headboard or footboard. Such a gap is wide enough for a child to fall through and get trapped or suspended. When this happens, a child – especially one on the upper bunk – could be strangled. Given this hazard, parents must never put a regular-length mattress on an extra-long bed.

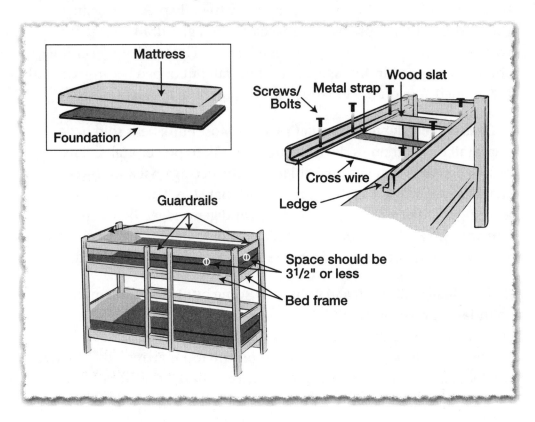

Safety tips for selecting and using bunk beds

Now let's cover some key guidelines for selecting a safe bunk bed and using it safely.

A safe bunk bed

A safe bunk bed has the following:

♦ Guardrails on both sides that are screwed or bolted to the bed frame

♦ Guardrails that extend at least 5 inches above the mattress surface

♦ Cross ties under the mattress foundation that won't come loose

♦ A secure ladder that won't slip when a child climbs on it

♦ A feature that lets you separate the upper and lower beds to form 2 single beds, in case you have a child too young to sleep safely on the upper bunk

♦ A mattress that fits the bed frame (i.e., both the same length)

Safety Note

Bunk Beds: Too Young for Top

For a growing family with limited room, bunk beds can be a practical benefit because they save space. But there's no getting around the fact that bunk beds pose some real safety dangers to young children. This being so, parents should never allow a child under age 6 to sleep on the upper bunk. Before age 6, children aren't developmentally far enough along to negotiate the top bunk hazards.

Safe use

Parents should take the following safe-use precautions with bunk beds:

+ Don't use the upper bunk unless it has guardrails on both sides.

+ Keep guardrails in place at all times, regardless of your child's age.

+ Don't permit a child under age 6 to sleep in the upper bunk.

+ Make sure there are cross-wire supports under the mattress foundation of both the upper and lower bunks.

+ Don't permit horseplay or rough-housing on or near the beds.

+ Teach children to use the ladder, and only the ladder, to climb in or out of the top bunk (i.e., no chairs or other furniture as substitute ladders).

+ Put a night light in the bedroom with the bunk beds so the child on top can see the ladder if she needs to get up during the night.

Parents also need to concern themselves with the placement of bunk beds in a room. The beds should be far enough from any windows that children can't reach them from top or bottom bunk. They also should be beyond the reach of window blind or drapery cords, which can be a strangulation danger. It's best not to put bunks against a wall with any hanging picture frames or shelves. And a set of bunks should never be situated anywhere near a ceiling fan. In fact, you're wisest to simply not have bunks in a room with a ceiling fan.

REVIEW OF KEY SAFETY POINTS

Let's summarize the key points presented in this chapter:

Setting Up the Crib

✔ Cover the mattress with a fitted bottom sheet.

✔ Place the crib well out of reach of window blinds or curtains cords.

✔ Don't put any soft or fluffy bedding in the crib.

✔ Don't hang items such as diaper bags or toys on the crib.

✔ Mount mobiles beyond the baby's reach.

✔ Trim any slack from crib bumper ties.

✔ Precautions to follow if tucking your baby in with a blanket:

- Use a thin blanket

- Put baby with her feet near foot of crib

- Pull blanket up no farther than baby's chest and tuck in edges

Putting Baby to Bed

✔ Dress your baby in snug-fitting, flame-resistant sleepwear once she can crawl (around 9 months old).

✔ Always place your baby to sleep on her back.

✔ Do not bring your baby into bed with you to sleep.

Crib Adjustments

✔ Lower the mattress to the middle setting and remove crib toys when your baby reaches 5 months or can push up on her hands and knees.

✔ Adjust the mattress to the lowest setting and remove crib bumper pads when your child can stand up.

✔ It's time to switch your child to a bed when she is approximately 35 inches tall or can scale the side of the crib.

Toddler and Bunk Beds

✔ Toddler beds are great for transitioning from the crib to a full-size bed.

✔ Don't allow a child under age 6 to sleep on the upper bunk of bunk beds.

✔ Make sure bunk beds have secure guardrails on all sides, cross-tie mattress supports, and proper-size mattresses.

✔ Teach children to use only the ladder to climb in or out of the top bunk.

✔ Place a night light in a bedroom with bunk beds so children can see the ladder at night.

We've reached the end of our lesson on sleep safety. Next, let's turn to safety issues with infant products.

Guide to Infant Products

As parent of an infant, consider yourself fortunate: There are many different baby products today that can make your life a little easier while satisfying the basic demands of caring for your baby. Things like changing tables, combination infant car seats/carriers, and portable playpens. Not to mention diaper pails that make "sausages" out of diapers! It wasn't so long ago that such items either didn't exist or weren't widely available to consumers. (As your parents like to point out to you at every opportunity!)

Nowadays, baby products provide a level of convenience that earlier generations of parents would very much envy. And even products which have been around for a long time – cribs, highchairs and strollers, for example – are generally better designed and more user-friendly today.

Convenience is a good thing in baby products. But keep in mind that it's always secondary to safety. The most important factor with any infant product is that it be safe for your baby. Fortunately, we know a lot more about child safety than did our parents' or grandparents' generations. This greater understanding in society has brought us infant products that meet stricter safety standards. But safer product design goes only so far in preventing mishaps. The key really is safe product *use*. Which means using an item as it was designed and built to be used.

Improper use of an infant product could put your baby at risk of injury – even very serious injury, depending on the product and circumstance. This is the last thing you want to happen. Infant product safety begins, then, with always following the manufacturer's instructions for safe assembly and use.

Let's have a general word about these instructions. After we do, we'll cover safety considerations for some of the most common infant products.

MANUFACTURER'S INSTRUCTIONS

Warning: when you begin buying baby products, be prepared for a lot of safety warnings. They're everywhere. On the box. On the product itself. Throughout the manufacturer's instructions or owner's manual. What's with all the warnings? Are baby products so unsafe? No, not exactly. The warnings are just a concession to a few realities about babies: They're especially vulnerable to product-use hazards. They can be very seriously hurt in product mishaps. And they're powerless to protect themselves from product dangers. As parents, we should be grateful for all the warnings. When heeded, they prevent injuries and protect lives.

Unfortunately, parents often don't follow the manufacturer's product warnings. Not because they defy them on purpose. Rather, they simply ignore or overlook them. Why? Maybe it's "warning overload." Whatever the reason, we know that misuse of baby products can and does result in serious injuries to infants and toddlers. And let's point out that these are *perfectly safe products*, when used as instructed.

Lots of parents also ignore the manufacturer's proper-use instructions for a product. Again, we pose the question: Why? It might have something to do with how poorly written and confusing many owner's manuals can be. But it also could be because parents assume 1) they know how a product is supposed to work; and 2) they're already aware of all the hazards it poses. This, on both counts, is a dangerous assumption. In so many cases, the possible dangers with infant products are ones that parents never would've foreseen without benefit of a warning.

The bottom line? Never ignore safety warnings on baby products. And always follow the manufacturer's instructions regarding safe use.

Our aim in this chapter is to raise parents' awareness of key safety aspects – hazards and use guidelines – for widely used infant products. The information we offer here is *not* meant to replace or modify the manufacturer's instructions for a particular product you own. If anything we say here seems to conflict with your manufacturer's instructions, go with what the manufacturer tells you to do (or not to do).

Before we get to specific products, let's have a word about the issue of used or second-hand products.

USED PRODUCTS

Parents on a budget may choose to acquire baby products used. They might accept hand-me-downs from family or friends. Or they could purchase items at a thrift store, consignment shop, or garage sale, or through a classified ad or online auction. There is a large second-hand market in, for example, cribs, bassinets, car seats, and strollers, among many other products.

If you plan to get anything used for your baby, be mindful of the following important safety issues:

+ A used product could have been recalled by the manufacturer at some point for being unsafe. So before acquiring or using a second-hand item, make sure it's never been subject to a product recall. (See Chapter 6 for details on how to determine a product's recall status.)

+ A used item often won't come with its original owner's manual or product guide. At some point, in change of ownership, the manual went permanently missing. This manual is important to have because it covers guidelines for safe product assembly and use. What to do if you're not provided with the original manual when you acquire a used product? Contact the manufacturer, who should be able to send you a replacement one.

Now we're ready to go over safety considerations for the following popular baby products:

+ Highchairs   + Toy chests

+ Changing tables   + Playpens

+ Infant carriers   + Strollers

+ Walkers   + Baby gates

► HIGHCHAIRS ◄

There's a reason they're not called low chairs. For the little people who sit in them, highchairs are high off the floor. And any time babies are elevated, there's the potential for accidental falls and injuries. Experience tells us that most highchair injuries happen when the restraining straps aren't used at all; when they're used incorrectly; or when the chair tips over. Fortunately, most highchair accidents are easily avoided through proper precautions.

Highchair Restraining Systems

The restraining system, as its name suggests, holds a baby in the seat. Failure to use the restraining straps at all is very dangerous because a child who isn't secured in the seat could stand up and topple over.

Safe highchairs have both waist and crotch restraining straps. These 2 straps, which together form a simple harness, keep your baby from slipping out of the chair. Always secure your infant in the chair with *both* waist and crotch restraints to ensure he stays put. Make sure the crotch strap, which runs between the legs, is attached securely to the waist strap. If it's not, your child could slip down beneath the tray, putting him at risk of strangulation on the waist strap. You also should adjust the waist strap so it's snug around his waist, so he can't stand up.

One mistake you never want to make is to use the highchair tray as a restraining device in lieu of the straps. The tray is not a safety feature; under no circumstance should it be used as a substitute for the restraining system.

Lastly, many older chairs have only a waist strap. The lack of a crotch strap makes these outdated chairs unsafe to use. If you own such a chair, you need to either dispose of it, or if possible, have it retrofitted with a crotch restraint.

Avoiding Tip-Overs

Tip-overs usually happen when a child in a highchair pushes off from a neighboring table or stands up in the chair. They happen, too, when the child rocks back and forth in the chair – or someone else (i.e., another child) rocks the chair to and fro with the child in it. These general tip-over scenarios can be prevented by following a few simple precautions:

+ Keep the highchair more than arm's distance from the nearest table or other surface your child might use to push off.

+ Strap your child in the chair so he can't stand up.

+ Don't let older kids hang on or otherwise play around the highchair when your little one's using it.

You can further minimize highchair risks by getting a chair with the following preventive features:

+ A wide base for stability. Avoid any model that rocks easily when you push on the seat from front to back or side to side.

+ A post between the legs. This feature provides extra protection against a child slipping under the tray.

✦ Wheels attached to the base. The wheels can stop a highchair from tipping over should the child in it push off from a table. How? By permitting the chair to roll backwards rather than topple.

✦ Vertical positioning adjustments. These let you lower the chair's center of gravity, and thus improve its stability, by positioning the seat closer to the ground.

If you happen to have a fold-up style highchair, you want to make sure the locking device is deployed each time you set up the chair. Overlooking this step could result in the chair collapsing while in use.

Be mindful that a highchair is not itself a safety device. So you should never leave your child alone or unsupervised when he's strapped in his highchair.

▷ CHANGING TABLES ◁

A changing table won't make changing a diaper fun. But it can make a diaper change easier to get through for the diaper changer. A table spares parents the strain of having to bend over during a change. It also offers them the convenience of being able to store diapers, wipes, and lotions within easy reach.

There are 2 main safety issues with changing tables. The first is proper restraint. Most injuries with these tables happen when children fall to the floor because they weren't secured with the safety straps. Make sure you always use the straps to restrain your child whenever he's on the table – for as long as he's on the table. And even when he's strapped down, you mustn't leave him there unattended because he could work his way out of the straps while you're away. Straps are crucial to changing table safe use. Any table without them, therefore, is unsafe to use.

The second main safety issue is accidental tip-overs. A changing table is a piece of furniture. As such, unless it's anchored properly, it may tip over if a child climbs on it. And if it does tip over, it's likely to fall on top of the climber. The key to preventing tip-overs is to make sure your changing table is stable. Stability begins with proper anchoring – to the wall, ideally. If your table has drawers, it should not lean noticeably when the drawers are open; if it does, it's not stable enough.

If your child is a super "wiggle worm," and strapping him to the changing table is a rodeo event, you should consider changing his diaper on a lower surface to avoid the risk of a fall. A simple alternative to using the table is to spread a towel on a bed or the floor.

▷ INFANT CARRIERS ◁

An infant carrier seat, with its handle for lifting, is convenient for transporting a baby from here to there, or simply for holding a baby when a parent's hands are otherwise busy. The product comes in 2 types: 1) a freestanding carrier; and 2) a combination infant-only car seat and carrier, which is 2 products in 1. (Infant-only car seats are covered at length in Chapter 8.)

What's great about the combination product is that the carrier feature lets you carry your baby to and from your car without having to unbuckle him or lift him from the seat. This is a wonderful thing if he's asleep in the carrier and you don't want to wake him.

These infant carriers can be hazardous if they're not used properly. You can help prevent accidents with your carrier by following a few simple precautions:

Safety Note

Infant Carriers and Restaurant Seating

You've probably walked into a family restaurant and seen the following: a baby still strapped in his infant carrier seat, which has been placed on an inverted wooden highchair. And you might have thought to yourself, "That's a nifty solution to seating a baby when out dining." Nifty, yes, in that the carrier fits conveniently into the base of the highchair. But unfortunately, not safe.

Resting an infant carrier on an inverted highchair endangers the baby in the carrier seat because the upside-down highchair is very unstable. An unintentional push or nudge by a waiter or other passerby is all it would take to topple the highchair and send the carrier seat — with the baby in it — to the floor.

The convenience of this seating arrangement is not worth the safety hazard it poses. An infant carrier with a baby in it needs to be on stable footing.

+ Always place the carrier on the floor before you insert or remove your baby.

+ Always use the belt restraints to secure your baby in the carrier.

+ Don't place the carrier atop furniture when your baby's in it. His movement in the seat could possibly tip it over.

- ✦ If you do rest it on a table or countertop, always stay within arm's reach of your baby. (And be aware that carriers slide more easily on slippery surfaces, such as glass and formica.)

- ✦ Never place a carrier on a soft surface, such as a sofa or bed, when your baby's in it. If the carrier tipped over, your little one could get trapped face down on the soft surface and suffocate.

When it comes to the 2 types of infant carriers, there's one other very important safety point to be mindful of: a freestanding carrier is NOT a child car seat and should never be used as one.

WALKERS

Babies love infant walkers. And from a baby's vantage point, what's not to love? A walker, which consists of a round wheeled base and rigid upper frame that holds a fabric seat, gives him freedom of movement. And the thrill of speed! From a safety standpoint, however, walkers are a menace. According to the Consumer Product Safety Commission, they send many thousands of children to hospital ERs each year with assorted injuries, including broken bones, burns, and head injuries. These mostly result from the greater mobility and reach babies have when they're in a walker. Infants in walkers are at risk of

- ✦ rolling down steps or stairs;

- ✦ tipping over when crossing uneven surfaces (such as door thresholds or carpet edges);

- ✦ pulling a hot beverage from a coffee or side table;

+ reaching a fireplace or radiator; or

+ falling into a pool, bathtub, or toilet.

The American Academy of Pediatrics (AAP) considers walkers to be so unsafe that it strongly advises against using them. The AAP points out that even close adult supervision won't prevent most walker accidents and the injuries they inflict because the supervisor simply can't respond fast enough. A child in a walker can move 3 feet in the space of a second! The AAP also dispels the popular belief, which many parents hold, that walkers help children to walk sooner. Not true, according to the AAP.

If you do choose to let your child use a walker, make sure it's one that meets the new safety standard established in 1997 to cut down on injuries. (It should have a label that says "Meets New Safety Standard.") This new standard requires a walker 1) to be wider so it can't fit through a standard doorway; and 2) to include a gripping mechanism to stop it at the edge of a step.

Before you ever let your baby in his "new-generation" walker, remove all plastic labels and decals from it and throw them away because they're a choking hazard. Do not, however, remove the permanent warning labels. And whenever your baby is going to use the walker, take the following precautions:

+ Close the door or safety gate at the top of any stairs.

+ Permit him to scoot around only on smooth surfaces.

+ Block his access to any water sources.

+ Don't let him out of your sight.

+ Make sure no hot surfaces (e.g., a radiator) or hot liquids (e.g., a bowl of soup on a tray stand) are reachable by him.

A much safer alternative to a walker is a stationary activity center, or entertainer, which has no wheels. No wheels mean no mobility. And no mobility eliminates nearly all the injury risks posed by walkers.

Toy Chests

Is your home starting to look like a toy store hit by a tornado? Toys everywhere! You can't take a step without landing on one. Where to keep them all? One simple solution is a toy chest. This popular item has been a staple of childhood for many generations.

If you own a toy chest, or plan to get one, you should be aware of the potential dangers they pose to little people. There are 2 main hazards:

1. **A falling lid:** This is the most common mishap with toy chests. The lid, if it's unsupported, can fall on a child as he's reaching into the chest. The falling lid might either hit him on the head or trap him by the neck. Experience tells us that falling lids can cause serious, even fatal, injuries.

2. **Lack of ventilation:** If a chest isn't properly ventilated, a child could suffocate if he climbed in it and got trapped with the lid closed.

Given these serious hazards, you should look for a toy chest with the following features:

- ✦ A hinged lid that stays open in any position

- ✦ No exterior latches on the lid which could close and entrap a child inside

- ✦ Good ventilation (either dedicated holes in the chest or a space between the lid and sides of the chest when the lid is closed)

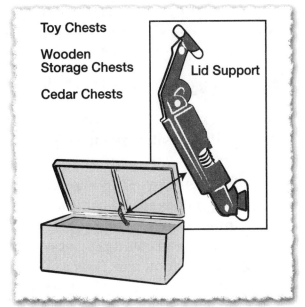

Toy Chests

Wooden Storage Chests

Cedar Chests

Lid Support

Suppose you own an older toy chest with a free-falling lid. How might you use it safely? Either remove the lid altogether, or install a spring-loaded lid support that will hold the lid open in any position.

Be mindful, too, that a household cedar chest or other wood chest, which parents sometimes will use as a makeshift toy storage container, is associated with the same safety risks as a toy chest.

PLAYPENS

You need to put your baby down for a while so you can get some household chores done. You'd like him to be close by, so you'd rather not put him in his crib in the nursery. Solution? A playpen, which is (or should be) a safe place for an infant or tot to play in or take a nap. Nowadays, playpens include play yards and so-called portable or travel cribs. Most models fold up for easy travel. A playpen's very portability puts a premium on setting it up correctly every time, according to the manufacturer's instructions. One that's set up wrong could collapse with the baby in it, resulting in serious injury – or worse.

Playpen Types

Playpens come in 3 basic types: wooden, drop sided, and hinged. Each has its key safety point for parents to be aware of:

- ✦ Wooden playpens – The slats should be spaced no more than 2³/8 inches apart – same as on a crib. Any wider, and an infant's body could squeeze through them; and if it did, the baby's head could get trapped against the slats, creating a strangulation risk. How can you check the spacing? Run the "soda can" test. Try to fit a soda can through the slats; if it slips through, the spacing is unsafe.

- ✦ Drop-sided playpens – Never leave an infant in a drop-sided playpen with the side down. When the side is lowered, the mesh hangs loose and forms a pocket in which a baby can become ensnared, putting the baby at risk of suffocation. Newer models have warning labels that alert parents to this hazard. Older drop-sided playpens, however, might not.

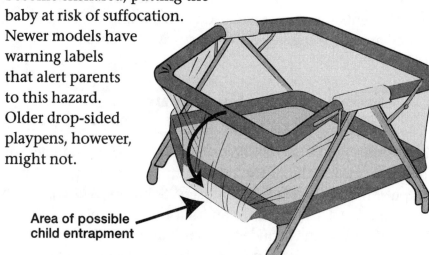

Area of possible child entrapment

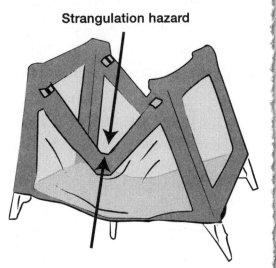

Strangulation hazard

✦ Hinged playpens – The collapsible hinges in the center of each top rail should lock automatically when lifted into the normal use position. If they don't, the rails could collapse and form a "V" shape. And a child's neck could get trapped in the "V," resulting in strangulation.

Mesh Netting

There's no escaping mesh with today's playpens. Nearly all drop-sided and hinged playpens have mesh netting for sides. Mesh presents some key safety issues, beyond the "pocketing" hazard we've already mentioned. Let's outline them:

✦ Mesh should have a weave of less than 1/4 inch so fingers, toes, and clothing buttons and snaps won't get snagged in the netting.

✦ A playpen with holes in the mesh is unsafe for use. Such holes are (or quickly become) a strangulation hazard.

✦ Check where the mesh attaches to the top rail and playpen floor for signs of loose threads or unraveling. A baby or toddler could get entangled in loose threads.

+ If the mesh is attached to the playpen floor with staples, make sure that none are loose or missing. Loose staples can cause an abrasion, while missing staples might leave an opening large enough to entrap a child's head.

Given the hazards just noted, it's a good idea to inspect a playpen's mesh netting frequently to make sure it's still in safe condition.

Safe Use

Whether putting your baby in a playpen for playtime or for a nap, there are some basic precautions you should follow for safe use:

+ Be very careful about attaching mobiles or toys to the playpen. No such item should ever be attached with a string or cord because it could pose a strangulation risk. For much the same reason, don't tie anything across a playpen or hang anything from its corners.

+ Don't place large toys in the playpen. A tot could use them to climb out.

+ Don't put your child in a playpen if he's dressed in loose-fitting clothes or is wearing a bib or necklace. These could catch on an item attached to the playpen or on raised hardware (a rivet, for example) and result in strangulation.

+ Never put your child in a playpen with a pacifier tethered to him with a string. The string could strangle him if it got wrapped around his neck.

A few additional precautions relate directly to nap time in a playpen:

✦ Always put a baby up to 1 year old to sleep on his back. As you'll recall from Chapter 4, sleeping on their back is safest for infants.

✦ Never put soft bedding of any kind in the playpen because of the suffocation hazard it poses. (See Chapter 4 for more information on safety considerations with soft bedding.)

✦ Use only the mattress pad that came with the playpen. Adding a mattress could create a suffocation hazard by forming spaces – either between mattresses, or between the added mattress and the side of the playpen – in which a slumbering infant or tot could get wedged.

STROLLERS

You'll spend lots of time, and log plenty of miles, chauffeuring your baby around in a stroller. So you'll want to be confident that the stroller is safe. For optimal safety, a stroller should have the following features:

✦ A wide wheel base and large wheels to prevent tipping over

✦ Brakes on 2 wheels (2 brakes are safer than 1)

✦ A safety belt and buckle that are securely fastened to the seat

Most injuries with strollers result when children fall from them. To prevent your baby from falling out, or from slipping down in the seat and getting trapped, always strap him in the stroller with the safety belt and buckle. And make sure the belt is a snug fit around your little one's waist.

You'll also want to take the following other use precautions:

+ Always park the stroller on level ground and apply the brakes *before* removing your baby.

+ Don't hang a pocketbook or bag over the handle bar because the weight could tip the stroller over.

+ Keep your child a safe distance from the stroller when either opening it or folding it up. Little fingers that find their way into a stroller's folding mechanism can get badly pinched or even amputated.

+ Never place soft, fluffy bedding in a stroller or use a blanket or pillow as a mattress because of the suffocation hazard they're know to pose to a napping baby. (See Chapter 4 for further information on the soft-bedding hazard with infants.)

+ You just bought a jogging stroller. Before you strap your little one in it and take off to pound the pavement, consult the man-ufacturer's recommended age, weight, and height minimums for safe use. The jostling and jolts that a passenger experiences in one of these strollers might be too much for a very young or very small baby.

One closing point before we move on to baby gates: As a practical safety matter, you should never leave your child unattended in a stroller. Not even briefly. You just never know what might happen while your baby is outside your supervision.

► BABY GATES ◄

Think infancy has its safety challenges? Wait until your baby starts crawling! Then he'll be able to roam wherever his curiosity leads him. And bank on the fact that it will lead him to hazardous places and situations. Once he is crawling, the best way to keep him from harm is to block his access to unsafe areas. Probably the most effective device for limiting his range of movement and keeping him from trouble is a baby gate, which usually is placed in doorways or at the top or bottom of stairs.

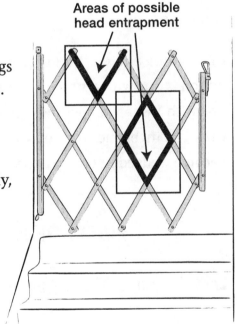

Areas of possible head entrapment

The old accordion-style gates, which have large V-shaped openings along the top and diamond-shaped openings between the slats, are very dangerous. The history with these gates tells us that a child's head can get trapped in the V- or diamond-shaped openings, resulting in strangulation. Fortunately, these accordion-style gates haven't been sold since 1985. But you still might run across one at a yard sale or in a thrift store. If you do, alert the owner and/or seller to the hazard it poses.

Nowadays, gates come in 2 main types: *permanent* and *pressure mounted*. Let's cover the key safety considerations with each.

Permanent gates are mounted directly on a wall or door jam with hardware. The extra safety benefit with these is that children, no matter how strong or determined, can't dislodge them or knock them over. A permanent gate, therefore, is what you want to install at the top of stairs or, say, at the entrance to an upstairs balcony.

Pressure-mounted gates are held in place by an adjustable pressure bar. These also are effective, and have the advantage of easy portability. But they may loosen or even dislodge if a child leans on or kicks or shakes them. (Which is why you shouldn't use one to block off stairs.) Make sure you always install a pressure-mounted gate with the pressure bar on the side away from your baby so he can't use it as a toehold to climb the gate.

In choosing a gate, either permanent or pressure mounted, your safest option is one with a straight top edge. But if you do consider getting one with V-shaped openings, make sure the openings are no more than 1 1/2 inches across. Any wider, and your child's head could become wedged in the V shapes.

REVIEW OF KEY SAFETY POINTS

Let's summarize the key points covered in this chapter:

Manufacturer's Instructions

    ✔ Never ignore the safety warnings on baby products.

    ✔ Always follow the manufacturer's instructions regarding safe use of infant products.

Used Products

✔ Check the recall status of used products before you purchase them to make sure they're safe.

✔ Be sure to obtain the manufacturer's product instructions for any used product you purchase.

Highchairs

✔ Highchairs should have both waist and crotch restraining straps.

✔ Always strap your baby in the chair with both waist and crotch restraints to prevent him from falling out.

✔ Never use the tray as a restraining device in lieu of the straps.

✔ Take precautions to prevent tip-overs:

- Keep highchair a safe distance from nearest table (so baby can't push off it)

- Keep older children away from chair when baby's in it

Changing Tables

✔ A table without restraining straps is unsafe.

✔ Always use the safety straps to restrain your child when he's on the table.

✔ Anchor the table properly (e.g., to the wall) to prevent tip-overs.

Infant Carriers

✔ The safest infant carrier has a sturdy base, skid-resistant bottom, and waist and crotch restraints.

✔ Always secure your baby in the carrier with the belt restraints.

✔ Never place a carrier on a soft surface (e.g., a sofa or bed) when your baby's still in it.

✔ Never use a freestanding carrier as a car seat.

✔ Never place an infant carrier with your baby in it on an inverted restaurant highchair.

Walkers

✔ The AAP advises against using walkers because they're so unsafe.

✔ Any walker you let your child use should meet the new safety standard established in 1997 to cut down on injuries.

✔ Remove all plastic labels and decals from your walker because they pose a choking hazard to your baby.

Toy Chests

✔ The 2 main hazards with toy chests are a falling lid (causing injuries) and inadequate ventilation (resulting in suffocation).

✔ A toy chest should have the following safety features:

- A hinged lid that stays open in any position

- A lid without exterior latches

- Proper ventilation

Playpens

✔ Slats on wooden playpens should be no more than 2³/₈ inches apart (wider spacing poses an entrapment/strangulation hazard).

✔ On hinged playpens, the collapsible hinges on the top rails should lock automatically when lifted into normal use position.

✔ Never leave an infant in a drop-sided playpen with the side down.

✔ Inspect mesh netting frequently to make sure it's still in safe condition.

✔ Never attach toys or mobiles to a playpen with a string or cord.

✔ Never place your baby in a playpen with a bib, necklace, or pacifier-on-a-string around his neck.

✔ Never put soft bedding in a playpen with your napping baby.

✔ Use only the mattress pad that came with the playpen.

Strollers

✔ A stroller should have the following safety features:

- Brakes on 2 wheels

- A safety belt and buckle that are securely fastened to the seat

✔ Always strap your baby in the stroller with the safety belt and buckle.

✔ Keep your child a safe distance from the stroller whenever opening it or folding it up (to prevent little fingers from getting pinched).

✔ Never place soft, fluffy bedding items in a stroller with your napping baby.

✔ Never use a blanket or pillow as a mattress beneath your napping baby.

Baby Gates

✔ Safety gates enable parents to block a baby's access to hazardous areas and objects.

✔ Old accordion-style gates are very dangerous because their V-shaped and diamond-shaped openings pose a strangulation hazard.

✔ Always use a permanent gate at the top of stairs.

✔ Always install a pressure-mounted gate with the pressure bar on the side away from your baby.

We've completed our safety guide to some of the most commonly used infant products. Next let's turn to the subject of product recalls.

CHAPTER 6

Product Recalls

Unfortunately, not all the products we buy for our babies and toddlers are necessarily safe. Inevitably, in our imperfect world, some items make it to store shelves with design flaws or manufacturing defects that make them unsafe. Every year, flawed children's products are responsible for many child accidents and injuries. These injuries can be serious, depending on the product and the safety hazard it poses. Product hazards are a major issue in child safety.

Fortunately, there's a system in place for alerting parents (as consumers) when a product is found to be unsafe. The cornerstone of the system is the product recall, which identifies the safety hazard or defect and instructs consumers what they need to do with the recalled item (e.g., repair or replace a defective part, or return the item to the manufacturer for a refund). For safety's sake, all parents need to be keen to product recalls. The well-prepared parent is one who understands how recalls happen; how to stay abreast of them; how to identify a recalled product; and why the recall system is less than perfect.

Our aim in this chapter is to introduce you to product recalls and explain how the recall system operates.

► How Products Are Recalled ◄

The federal government has a system for identifying and recalling hazardous consumer products. Several government agencies are responsible for recalls, depending on the product. The majority of children's products – nursery equipment, household items, toys, etc. – come under the jurisdiction of the Consumer Product Safety Commission (CPSC), which oversees some 15,000 consumer goods of all types. Jurisdiction over child car seats belongs to the National Highway Traffic Safety Administration (NHTSA), which is part of the US Department of Transportation.

When either the CPSC or NHTSA determines a product to be unsafe, it notifies the manufacturer. In turn, the manufacturer issues a recall announcement, alerting consumers to the product hazard and instructing them what to do about it. The item might require repair; or it might need to be replaced altogether. The safety oversight agencies may ban a product from the market if it is particularly dangerous and no reasonable safety standard can be established to protect consumers from it.

► Consumer Awareness (or Lack of It) ◄

When a product is officially recalled, retail stores are required to remove it from their shelves so consumers can no longer purchase it. Consumers in the market for a new item, therefore, are at no risk of acquiring something that's been recalled as hazardous. So a product recall really is no concern for these consumers, who are protected by the recall system, regardless of their awareness of any given recall.

Whom does the recall truly concern?

+ Consumers who bought the product before it was recalled. How many consumers this amounts to depends on the number of units that were sold prior to the recall. Depending on the product, the number could run into the thousands, hundreds of thousands – or even higher.

+ Consumers who buy the product second hand (at a thrift shop or garage sale, for example, or through an online auction) at some point after it's been recalled.

Experience tells us that these consumers very often don't know about the recall. And their lack of awareness means they risk continued use of an unsafe product. News of the recall never reaches them, for one or another reason. The person who bought an item a few years before the recall might not have filled out and submitted the product registration card, which is the tool most manufacturer's use to notify purchasers of a product recall. In many cases, products don't even come with a registration card. And as for used products, whoever buys one in all likelihood has no clue about its recall status. Why? Because an official recall notice doesn't follow a product around when it changes hands.

The "awareness gap" in product recalls is bad news for child safety. Across America, there are vast numbers of unsafe baby and toddler products still in use, or still circulating through a second-hand market, because parents and other caregivers don't realize these products were recalled. Every one of them poses a danger – in some cases, a very serious danger – to the child who uses it.

Are you unknowingly using a recalled infant or toddler product in your home? Are you sure? Let's outline the steps you can take to make certain no hazardous products are lurking under your roof.

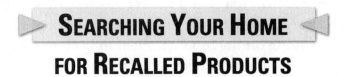

SEARCHING YOUR HOME FOR RECALLED PRODUCTS

Staying on top of product recalls takes time and effort. Consider it time and effort well spent – after all, your child's safety could be at stake. Making sure your little one isn't exposed to any recalled products involves 2 steps: 1) Identifying what children's products you own; and 2) Determining if any have been recalled.

Child Product Inventory

It doesn't take long to accumulate a lot of children's products. It usually happens even before a baby arrives, as many expecting parents will vouch. (Just ask them after their baby shower!) As parents accumulate ever more stuff for their baby, they can lose their handle on what they've got. One simple way to keep track of your multiplying children's items is to catalog them as you get them. Keep a running product inventory. This list should include the following information on each item:

+ Product type (e.g., strollers, beds and cribs, child car seats)

+ Manufacturer's name

+ Model number

+ Date purchased

+ Place of purchase

Such an inventory can greatly simplify a product recall check in your home. Whenever you hear of a recalled baby or toddler item – in the news, through a friend, at your pediatrician's office, or via the Internet – you can quickly check your list to see if it applies to you. For manageability's sake, it's best to start this product inventory as soon as you begin accumulating stuff, which is bound to be before your baby leaves the womb. But don't let a late start discourage you from taking inventory. It's worth your time and effort to go through all your baby products and get them cataloged.

See Appendix B for a sample Child Product Inventory Form. This tool should help you get organized to start cataloging.

Identifying Recalls

Your next step is to identify any recalls among products you own. Where do you go for product recall information? One source is the news. Now and then, a major child product recall gets reported in the national news. It's usually when the scope of the recall or seriousness of the hazard is too great to ignore. But the overwhelming majority of recalls never make it on the evening news. So the news media is, at best, a very limited information source on product recalls.

Let's consider these more viable ways to learn about product recalls: through product registration; and via the Internet.

Product Registration

Whenever you buy an item for your child, make sure you promptly complete the product registration card and return it to the manufacturer. Registering the product in this way enables the manufacturer to notify you in case the product ever gets recalled. Receiving this recall alert directly from the manufacturer assures that you won't be left in the dark about the presence in your home of a hazardous product.

The Internet

Say you forgot to submit a product registration card when you bought your baby's crib. (Lord knows where the card ended up!) Or suppose you purchased a bed guardrail that had no registration card. (Not every child's product does.) This much we know: You won't be directly notified by the manufacturers if either of these products ever gets recalled. How else might you find out their recall status? Go online. The Internet is a great resource for recall announcements. The CPSC and NHTSA websites provide extensive listings of products recalls. And many if not most manufacturers have websites where recall information is available on their products. Some websites send out recall announcements or updates by email to visitors who sign up for this service.

The most helpful online product recall databases include photos of the recalled items. There's just no substitute for a picture when you're trying to figure out if the product you own is the recalled product in question. This is especially true if you don't know your product's manufacturer or model number.

See Appendix D for guidance on locating websites where product recall notices and related information are available.

Keep in mind that you need to be proactive about product recalls. Don't expect recall information to magically find you. You need to take the initiative and do your homework.

Hazards by Product Categories

We can learn a lot about product safety hazards from the long record of children's product recalls. The fact is that products in a particular category (highchairs, pacifiers, strollers) tend to get recalled for similar reasons. Which isn't surprising, if you think about it. After all, products that share a category share similar designs, are built similarly, and have many common features. So it stands to reason that they

NEWS from CPSC

U.S. Consumer Product Safety Commission

Office of Information and Public Affairs   Washington, DC 20207

FOR IMMEDIATE RELEASE   **Company Phone Number: 800-345-4109**
Originally issued November 17, 1999   CPSC Consumer Hotline: (800) 638-2772
Last revised January 7, 2003   CPSC Media Contact: Nychelle Fleming, (301) 504-7063
Release # 00-019   Century Contact: Barbara Riggins, (610) 884-8490

**Note: Repair kit no longer available, but cash reward is still being offered.
Do not use these products. Please discard or destroy these products.**

Century Offers Cash Reward for Recalled Infant Swings
Four strangulation deaths reported

WASHINGTON, D.C. – In cooperation with the U.S. Consumer Product Safety Commission (CPSC) Century Products Co., of Macedonia, Ohio, offered a $30 cash reward for the repair of each Lil' Napper infant swing. These swings were recalled in 1997 following reports of three deaths and one near strangulation from entanglement in the swing's shoulder harness straps. CPSC and Century have since become aware of a fourth death to an 8-month old infant girl in Texas.

The swings, which were manufactured by Century from 1991 through 1997, have shoulder harness straps that are placed over each shoulder and buckled between the infant's legs. If the straps on these swings loosen or are unbuckled, an infant can become tangled in the straps and strangle.

Despite a nationwide effort over the past 2 years to alert the public about this recall, Century believes that many of the 125,000 swings originally sold could still be in use. Century took steps to get the word out, including direct mail notification to thrift stores and notices in new infant and convertible car seats.

The recalled Lil' Napper infant swings can be identified by the following model numbers, located on the bottom of the swing's seat: 12-344, 12-345, 12-347, 12-475 or 12-476. The Century brand name is on the motor assembly at the top of the swing. Each swing has a plastic, two-position seat with a removable plastic tray. The sets are covered by either a vinyl or fabric seat pad. There are four white tubular metal legs supporting the swing.

The repair program is no longer available. Parents and caregivers should immediately stop using these infant swings and discard or destroy the product. For more information, consumers can call the company's customer service number at 800-345-4109. If you have one of these swings, however, Century is still offering the $30 cash reward to compensate for having to discard or destroy the product.

would have similar safety flaws and pose similar hazards. In fact, research on children's product recalls over a recent 10-year period reveals clear hazard patterns for various product types. The hazards, by product category, are as follows:

Clothing

+ Choking hazard from detached fasteners, buttons, snaps, and other accessories

+ Burn hazard with clothing (especially sleepwear) that doesn't meet federal standards for fire protection

+ Lead poisoning hazard from buttons or fasteners that contain lead paint

Highchairs

+ Falling hazard due to defective restraining straps or bars

Infant carrier seats (freestanding or infant-only car seat carriers)

+ Falling hazard due to faulty handles that break when carrying a baby

Soft and backpack carriers

+ Falling hazard due to faulty harness

+ Strangulation hazard due to faulty harness

Pacifiers and teethers

+ Choking hazard if the nipple separates from the shield or the pacifier breaks into small parts

+ Suffocation hazard from lack of ventilation holes in the pacifier shield

+ Strangulation hazard if the pacifier is attached or tethered to a necklace or string

Play yards/Playpens

+ Entrapment and strangulation hazard from protruding hardware (dangerous catch points on which loose clothing might snag)

+ Strangulation hazard with a collapsed playpen; a baby's neck can get trapped between collapsed playpen rails

+ Choking hazard with small items detaching from the product (e.g., rail caps, locking posts, and unraveling mesh)

Strollers

+ Falling hazard due to faulty or broken restraint buckles

Swings

+ Falling hazard due to either faulty restraints or swing set instability (i.e., prone to tipping over)

+ Entanglement and strangulation hazard from faulty restraints

Toys

+ Choking hazard from small detached parts or broken pieces

+ Laceration hazard from sharp parts

Awareness of these hazard patterns could help you to identify items around your home that might be dangerous, regardless of whether they've ever been recalled. You don't have to wait for an official recall to remove something that appears unsafe, and which the recall history for the product category suggests may well be hazardous.

Safety Note

A Recalled Car Seat Safer Than No Seat at All

You just found out your toddler's car seat was recalled for a minor defect. You're worried about letting her still ride in the seat until you get it repaired. But you have no back-up seat in which to put your tot in the meantime. What to do? Is securing her in your car with a seat belt a safe option for the time being? Absolutely not!

According to the NHTSA, in the event you have no other seat, your best course is to continue to use the recalled car seat while you're waiting to get it repaired. Research shows that a recalled car seat is virtually always safer for your child than strapping her in with a safety belt.

IDENTIFYING A RECALLED PRODUCT: NOW WHAT?

So you think you've found a recalled item among your children's products. What do you do? Here are the steps you should undertake:

1. To start, you need to verify your suspicion by locating the official recall notice for the product. You should be able to find it online, either at the manufacturer's website, or at the website for the government

agency with jurisdiction for the product (CPSC or NHTSA).

2. Once you find the recall notice, confirm that it's for your product make and model number. Pay close attention to the product code and manufacturing date. An accurate confirmation usually depends on them.

3. Once you verify the recall, determine what's wrong with your product and how serious the problem is. Some recalls involve only minor defects; others are for major safety flaws. How serious the problem is with your product will determine if you can let your child continue to use it until you repair or replace it, whichever the recall requires. The recall notice should advise whether or not the product is still safe to use.

Take the example of a highchair that was recalled because it posed an entrapment hazard in the reclined position. But the chair was still safe to use when not reclined, as the recall notice specified. So, in this case, the product could still be used under limited circumstances until it got repaired.

4. Finally, redeem the recall by following the manufacturer's instructions for either repairing or replacing your product.

REVIEW OF KEY SAFETY POINTS

Let's summarize the key points covered in this chapter:

- ✔ Every year, children's products of all types get recalled for being hazardous.

- ✔ Each year, recalled products are responsible for numerous injuries involving young children.

✔ The federal government has a system for identifying and recalling hazardous products that threaten public safety.

✔ Understanding the recall process helps parents to protect their children from product hazards.

✔ Parents must take the initiative in identifying recalled children's products in their home.

✔ Parents must redeem any product recall that affects them (and therefore their child) by following the manufacturer's instructions for repairing or replacing the product.

This concludes our overview of product recalls. In the coming 3 chapters, we turn our attention to one of the most important topics in all of child safety: car seats. Let's begin with a general introduction to the key safety issues and considerations.

CHAPTER 7

Introduction to Car Seats

Car seats enter your life as soon as you become a parent. Indeed, hospitals won't discharge a newborn unless the parents have a suitable car seat in which to secure him. And all states have laws requiring car seats for children.

We transport our young kids by car all the time. That's life. And we understand that auto accidents can and do happen suddenly and without warning. Therefore, it's not hard to see why the car seat is so indispensable to child safety.

But many parents become frustrated with car seats, for understandable reasons. It seems like nothing about a car seat is easy. First, you have to choose the right one for your child among various different types. Then you have to install it, which can drive even the handiest parent to pull his or her hair out. And finally, you have to secure your little one correctly in the seat, which often involves a tricky adjustment of straps, harness, or snaps. The problem with frustration is that it can lead parents to become lax about car seats. And that's always bad for safety. You need to be mindful that your child's protection depends on you selecting the right seat, installing it correctly, and using it properly.

It would be hard to overstate the importance of car seat safety. Research shows that seat restraints dramatically reduce child fatalities in accidents when installed and used correctly.

We'll cover the car seat options available to you in the next chapter. Then in Chapter 9, we'll explain how to properly install and use car seats. But first, let's introduce you to some important general safety information about car seats.

CAR SEAT REGISTRATION

It seems like every time you buy something nowadays, the manufacturer is trying to get personal information about you as a consumer for its marketing purposes. The tool of choice for gathering information is the product registration card. Many of us ignore these cards because they have become intrusive. If you're likely to discard them, you should make an exception for your car seat registration card. Completing and submitting it is worth your effort.

Registering your car seat not only validates any product warranty; it also enables the manufacturer to notify you should your child's seat get recalled for any safety reason. Car seats are among the nearly 400 products that get recalled every year for safety flaws or defects. Car seats are not recalled as often as other products for kids, such as toys. But the scope of a car seat recall can be enormous. One such recall, for example, might affect hundreds of thousands of families.

So your first step after purchasing a car seat should be to fill out the registration card and mail it to the manufacturer. Do this before you throw out the box. You also should be sure to keep the owner's manual because you will need to refer to it during the installation process. Many car seats have a built-in compartment in which to store the manual.

Too Late to Register?

Suppose you bought a car seat and either discarded or lost the manufacturer's registration card. Now you're reading this and decide you want to register your purchase. Is it too late to do so? No, fortunately. You may still register your car seat through the National Highway Traffic Safety Administration (NHTSA), which is a part of the US Department of Transportation. Doing so will ensure that you receive notification in the event of a product recall. The registration form is available at the NHTSA website. Please see Appendix D for directions on locating this and other helpful child safety resources online.

▷ USED CAR SEATS ◁

Having kids is a costly deal, right from the start. Every time you turn around, there's another expense staring you in the face – be it diapers, formula, stuff for the nursery, pediatrician's visits, etc. And parents with older kids will tell you, "It never ends!" If money were no issue, then the cost of things wouldn't matter. But for most parents with young kids, money is an issue, and they're just looking for ways to economize without compromising safety.

One way to stretch your kiddie dollar is to buy items used, from thrift stores or consignment shops, at a garage sale or through an online auction. Today, there's a large second-hand market in baby/children's products, including car seats. Better still for the pocketbook is to inherit such items from family or friends, as part of a "hand-me-down" or "pass-it-along" network. Given the cost of car seats, the used option can be a relief for parents on a tight budget.

But economizing can't be at the expense of safety. A used seat is no bargain if it's unsafe. Anyone in the market for a second-hand seat needs to be aware of 2 general safety issues with used car seats. The first is recall status – was a used seat ever recalled by the manufacturer for safety reasons? If so, did the previous owner answer the recall and get the problem corrected? Chances are that the seller won't have the answers to these questions. Therefore, before you ever acquire a second-hand seat, you should check its recall status to make sure it's safe. (For further information on product recalls, see Chapter 6.)

The second issue is crash history. Has a used seat ever been involved in a vehicle crash? If so, depending on the seriousness of the crash, it might have been damaged, making it potentially unsafe for continued use. The NHTSA actually used to advise against using a seat that had been involved in a crash. It recently changed its position, however. It now says re-use of car seats after a *minor* crash is OK.

The NHTSA defines a crash as "minor" if it fits these criteria:

+ Air bags did not deploy.

+ No one was injured.

+ The vehicle door nearest the child safety seat was undamaged.

+ The vehicle in which the car seat was installed was drivable from the crash site.

+ A visual inspection under the seat padding reveals no cracks caused by the crash.

The problem for a consumer about to buy a second-hand seat is that he or she has no reliable way of determining its crash history – whether it was in a crash, for starters; and if it was, whether the crash was serious.

Given these uncertainties about a used seat's safety status, we recommend generally that parents avoid going the second-hand route. At the least, you should acquire a used seat only from someone you know and whom you're confident can vouch for the seat's recall and crash record. Otherwise, you could unknowingly end up with an unsafe seat that puts your child at greater risk of harm.

➤ CHILD CAR SEAT COMPATIBILITY ◄

There are numerous models of car seats, made by various manufacturers. There also are many makes and models of passenger vehicles. Plus there is a variety of vehicle seat belt systems. It's not surprising, then, that not every child seat can be installed in all vehicles and all seating positions. The best way to ensure that your child's seat will be compatible with your vehicle is to test install the seat before you purchase it.

➤ WHO'S BUCKLING IN YOUR CHILD? ◄

During the years your child rides in a car seat, there are bound to be times when someone other than you must secure him in the seat. It might be a babysitter or nanny; a grandparent; the parent of a playmate; or someone with whom you take part in a carpooling arrangement.

Given that 4 out of 5 parents and other caregivers install and use car seats incorrectly, you need to be very careful about entrusting anyone else with responsibility for buckling in your child. (See Chapter 9 for details on the incidence of improper installation and use.) Make sure that any such person knows how to do it correctly.

▷ DRIVE SAFELY ◁

Let's point out the obvious – your little one cannot get injured in an auto accident so long as you're not involved in one. And your likelihood of being in a crash is certainly a function of how carefully you drive. You can't control what others do on the road. But you can control your own behavior behind the wheel.

Before we get to driving safety on the road, let's mention a key preventive step to take before you ever leave the driveway with your child in back.

Secure Loose Objects

Before pulling out, check your vehicle for loose cargo. Groceries, children's products, even pets can become dangerous projectiles during a crash or sudden stop if they're not properly secured. It's estimated that children get struck by loose objects inside the car in 15% of collisions. Be aware that loose cargo can inflict serious injuries in the event of a crash. If your vehicle has a trunk, store as many unsecured items as possible in it. If you drive a minivan, SUV, or station wagon, be sure to install a cargo net or divider between passenger and storage areas to protect all passengers.

Distractions

We know that driver distraction is a major cause of accidents. This being the case, you must do your best to eliminate distractions while driving with your child aboard. The following rank among the most notorious distractions for parents in the driver's seat:

Cell Phones – As hectic as your life is, you like to optimize your time when you're driving. So maybe you use it to fit in some phone calls on your cell phone. Smart time management? Yes. But a safe thing to do? No – definitely not. Behind the wheel is no place to multitask! Never use a cell phone while driving. Speaking on a hand-held phone distracts your focus from the road and leaves you with only one hand on the wheel. The clear safety hazard cell phones pose has led some states to ban their use by drivers. If you must make a call from behind the wheel, do so *before* you pull out on the road or *after* you pull off the road and park safely.

Toys – Kids love toys. Kids drop toys. Some kids drop toys in cars and scream until you pick them up. The screaming is enough of a distraction. The situation gets worse if you, the driver, try to reach in the back seat to retrieve a toy while continuing to drive. Very bad idea. Doing so puts you and your screaming child at much greater risk of being in an accident. Either tune out the screaming, or pull safely off the road before fetching a toy from the back seat.

Music – Some infants and toddlers can get very picky about the music they like to listen to. Find a radio station or CD they find enjoyable and stick to it. This will eliminate the need to be changing CDs or radio stations while driving.

Hair/Make up – Peeking in the rear view mirror in order to fix your hair or make up diverts your attention from the road. Remember – it only takes a moment's lapse in attention to end up in an accident. Always wait until you stop the car and park safely before tending to your hair or make up.

Eliminating distractions such as these will make for safer driving when your little one is your passenger. Keep your focus on the road!

Don't Leave Child Unattended

You reach your destination and park your car. You then notice your child is asleep in back. You only need to do a quick errand. Rather than wake your child up, you consider leaving him in the locked vehicle while you run your errand. Bad idea. You should simply never leave your child unattended in your car, even when he is strapped in his seat. A child left alone is vulnerable to heat or cold inside an enclosed vehicle, depending on the season. We've all heard awful accounts of young children who got ill – or worse – from heat exposure because they were left inside an air-tight vehicle on a hot day.

A MATTER OF DIRECTION: REAR FACING AND FORWARD FACING

A quick preliminary word about the direction of car seats when installed: Some face to the *rear*. Some face *forward*. The difference in direction is dictated by safety factors tied to the age and physical development of children under 8 years of age. We will cover rear- versus forward-facing seats, including the safety rationale for each, in the coming 2 chapters.

REVIEW OF KEY SAFETY POINTS

Let's summarize the key points covered in this chapter:

✔ Car seats greatly reduce child fatalities in accidents when installed and used correctly.

✔ Register your child's car seat with the manufacturer so you'll receive notification of any product safety recalls.

✔ A used seat is considered safe as long as it hasn't been involved in a major crash, as defined by the NHTSA. Acquire a used seat only from someone you know and trust to vouch for the seat's acceptable crash history.

✔ Determine the recall status of a second-hand seat before you acquire it.

✔ Avoid purchasing a car seat at a thrift shop, consignment store, garage sale or online auction.

✔ Drive safer by eliminating driver distractions.

✔ Never leave your child unattended in your vehicle.

That's all for our introduction to car seats. Next, we outline the different car seat options available to parents with young children.

CHAPTER

8

Car Seat Options

A child's introduction to car seats comes as soon as her proud parents leave the hospital with her. She will log countless miles in a succession of seats as she progresses through early childhood. These different seats will mark her growth and development, providing the protection she needs as she goes from infancy to toddlerhood to her pre-kindergarten years and beyond. The protective requirements for riding safely will change as she grows. Which is why she must graduate from one type of seat to the next.

There are a few general types of car seats available to parents with young children. These different seats are designed for different age and corresponding developmental ranges. Our aim in this chapter is to introduce parents to their car seat options and help them select the right seat for their child. We'll cover the various seat types for children. They are the following: *infant only; convertible; forward facing;* and *boosters*. We'll go over safety considerations with each and outline advantages and disadvantages.

➤ WHICH SEAT, AND WHEN? ◄

The different types of car seats are grouped broadly by the direction which they face in when they're installed – either to the *rear* or *forward*. The difference in direction is a function of safety dynamics related to a child's age and physical development. (We cover the safety rationale for rear versus forward facing in further detail in Chapter 9.) Here is the breakdown by direction:

Rear-facing seats	Forward-facing seats
Infant only	Convertible (forward-facing position)
Convertible (rear-facing position)	Forward facing
	Booster

Let's go over the seat types, one after the next, so you have a clear picture of each and are well equipped to select the right one for your child.

➤ INFANT-ONLY SEATS ◄

This rear-facing seat is designed for infants from birth to approximately 1 year of age. Children who are older than 1 should continue to ride in the seat so long as they haven't reached its mandated weight limit, which generally is 20 to 22 pounds. An infant-only car seat is 2 products in 1: a child safety seat and an infant carrier. The seat has a handle attachment that's used for carrying your baby outside the car.

There are 2 options with the infant-only seat:

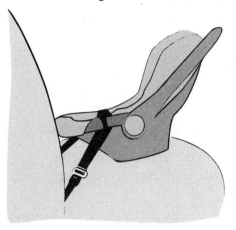

Infant-Only Seat Without Base

1. Without a base: The seat minus a base is the original configuration for this seat type. No base means the seat gets attached directly to the vehicle seat.

2. With a base: It's the same seat, only it comes with a companion base, which affixes to your vehicle's back seat. The infant-only seat then snaps into the base unit.

Advantages

This seat type, with or without a base, offers the following advantages:

+ Convenience – The carrier feature lets you secure your baby in the seat and then transport her easily between your home (or wherever else you might be) and your car. And this can be especially useful when your baby falls asleep in the car, as babies tend to do. Many models have companion strollers to make traveling easier.

+ Size – The infant-only seat has a smaller shell, which permits a better fit for younger infants. It also eliminates need for additional head support for most newborns.

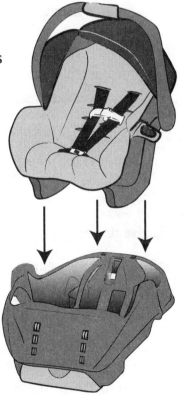

Infant-Only Seat With Base

✦ Sun visor – Though not safety related per se, this feature can come in handy when the sun is shining bright and you want to shield your baby from it.

The seat with base offers several additional advantages:

✦ Easy "snap on" installation – Once the base unit is strapped to your vehicle's back seat, all you need to do is insert the seat/carrier (with your baby already secured in it) in the base. It's a snap!

✦ Use with multiple vehicles – By purchasing bases for each of your vehicles, you can use the infant-only seat in any of them, hassle free.

✦ Adjustable base – Some models have an adjustable base to allow proper seat positioning without need for towels or foam inserts.

✦ Middle position – The seat with base is the most convenient model for placement in the middle (i.e., safest) position in the back seat.

Disadvantages

The infant-only seat, with or without a base, poses the following disadvantage:

✦ "Life span" – These seats have a weight limit generally between 20 and 22 pounds. So depending on your child's size, she might outgrow it in under a year. Which means you then would have to purchase a convertible seat before her first birthday.

Other disadvantages correspond to whether or not the seat has a base:

+ A seat without a base requires you to re-install the seat in your vehicle every time you've used it as a baby carrier.

+ A seat with a base has 2 points of attachment (base to vehicle, via the seat belt system; and infant seat to base, via the base unit's locking mechanism) whereas other seat types have a single point of attachment. Two points means double the number of attachments that could experience a glitch.

⮞ CONVERTIBLE SEATS ⮜

The convertible type seat has seat settings and seat belt paths that allow it to be either rear or forward facing. This seat can generally be used from birth to 40 pounds, or roughly 4 years of age. The seat is initially used in the rear-facing position then converted to the forward-facing position when the child is older than 1 year and exceeds the seat's rear-facing weight limit.

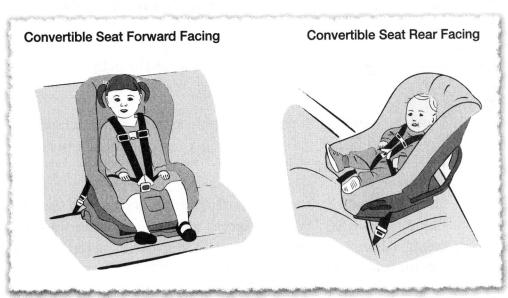

Convertible Seat Forward Facing   **Convertible Seat Rear Facing**

Advantages

The convertible seat offers a couple of distinct advantages:

- Cost-effective – Because of its convertibility (from rear to forward facing), the seat is good for approximately 4 years, which spares you from having to buy another seat when your baby becomes a toddler.

- Twist-resistant straps – The convertible seat's harness straps tend to be wider and thicker, and therefore less prone to twisting (hooray!). Wider also means more surface area to absorb impact forces in a crash when the seat is forward facing.

Disadvantages

The convertible seat also poses some disadvantages:

- Less convenient – Unlike the infant-only seat, it stays in the vehicle and can't be used as an infant carrier. So parents must unbuckle and lift their baby from the seat every time they remove her from their vehicle.

- Size – The seat shell is bigger, which means the baby passenger may need added head support in her first few months.

- Harness "misfit" – Models with padded shield harnesses sometimes won't fit newborns properly because the shield rests too high on the baby.

- Strap positioning – The harness straps must go through the highest slots (which are reinforced) when the seat is forward facing. Parents must remember to do this when converting from rear to forward facing.

Rear-Facing Car Seats

Advantages	Infant Only Without Base	Infant Only With Base	Convertible
Convenience		✗	
Better fit (for infants)	✗	✗	
Sun visor	✗	✗	
Ease of installation		✗	
Cost-effective (4 years of use)			✗
Wider straps to resist twisting			✗

▷ REAR-FACING RECOMMENDATION ◁

While all of the rear-facing seat options provide adequate protection, the infant-only seat with base provides the most convenience to you and your baby because of its *easy installation* (it's a snap!) and *mobility* (seat and carrier in one).

Once you decide on the type of seat you want, you should select a model with a heavier rear-facing weight limit. This higher weight ceiling lets you keep your baby rear facing longer, which is a good thing because rear facing is the safest position.

For help in selecting a rear-facing car seat, you can consult the NHTSA's Car Seat Ease of Use Ratings for Infant-Only and Convertible Seats, which is available at the NHTSA website. Please see Appendix D for guidance on locating this and other helpful online child safety resources.

Safety Note

Car Seats for "Premies"

Babies born prematurely (i.e., before 37 weeks) may have breathing problems because their lungs aren't yet fully developed. If your baby is such a "premie," you may not be able to use infant-only or convertible car seats at first because your newborn can't sit in a semi-reclined position. If so, your pediatrician may instruct you to use a car bed until your baby is breathing without complications.

▷ FORWARD-FACING SEATS ◁

Forward-Facing Seat With 5-Point Harness

This seat type, which is used forward facing only, is designed for children who weigh from 20 to 40 pounds.

Parents should be aware that there are 3 harness types available for a forward-facing seat:

1. **5-point harness** – This comprises 5 straps (2 shoulder straps, 2 hip straps, and 1 crotch strap) that converge and buckle together at a single point at the child's waist. Many safety experts recommend this type because the hip straps fit over a child's strong hip bones to

secure her snugly in the seat. The straps can be readily adjusted to fit smaller and larger children alike.

2. **T-shield harness** – With this type, the shoulder straps are attached to a T-shaped pad or shield, which snaps into a buckle at the crotch.

3. **Tray-shield (or overhead) harness** – With this type, the shoulder straps are attached to a tray-like overhead padded shield that swings down into position. The straps extending from the tray shield snap into a buckle at the crotch.

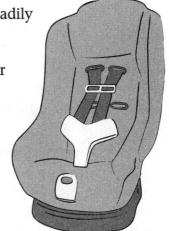

Forward-Facing Seat With T-Shield Harness

Advantages

The forward-facing seat presents a couple of advantages:

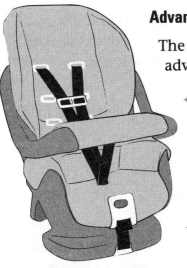

Forward-Facing Seat With Tray Harness

* Harness strap versatility – The harness straps can go through the harness slots at any setting. By contrast, a convertible seat's harness straps must be positioned at the highest slot setting when the seat is forward facing.

* Wider and thicker harness straps – The straps on a forward-facing seat, like those on a convertible seat, are wider and thicker so they're less prone to getting twisted. Wider also means more surface area to absorb impact forces in a crash.

Disadvantage

Be aware that the T-shield and tray-shield harnesses may not provide the same level of support in the area of the child's hips as does the 5-point harness.

▷ BOOSTER SEATS ◁

A booster seat is the transitional safety restraint for children who've outgrown a forwarding-facing seat but aren't old or big enough to be secured solely by the vehicle's seat belt. In many states, children are required to ride in a car seat only up to age 4 or so. Thus, many parents assume, mistakenly, that it's safe to strap their child in their vehicle with just the seat belt once she reaches age 4 or 5. The fact is that a seat belt, by itself, is not designed for kids so young and small. The vehicle's seat belt *is* used to restrain children once they reach 40 pounds – but only in combination with a booster seat.

A booster, as its name suggests, boosts a seated child to a height that makes it safe to use the seat belt to restrain her. Sitting in the booster, the child becomes tall enough for the seat belt to fit across her properly and protect her as it's supposed to.

There are 2 types of booster seats available to parents: the no-back belt-positioning booster; and the high-back belt-positioning booster.

No-Back Belt-Positioning Booster Seat

The no-back belt-positioning booster is designed for use in vehicles with built-in head restraints. The child is restrained in the seat using the vehicle's seat belt. Thus, this seat type is suitable for children only when they've reached 40 pounds.

High-Back Belt-Positioning Booster Seat

This seat type has the virtue of versatility – it can serve as either a forward-facing toddler seat or booster seat. The high-back belt-positioning seat comes with a removable 5-point harness, which is used to restrain child passengers when they weigh from 20 to 40 pounds.

Once a child reaches 40 pounds (usually around age 4), the harness is removed and the seat is converted to a belt-positioning booster seat. In the belt-positioning mode, the child is restrained in the seat with the vehicle's seat belt, which is inserted through the positioning slots on the booster seat's upper sides.

High-Back Booster Seat With 5-Point Harness

Advantage

The high-back booster seat with 5-point harness is an economical choice for parents because of its extended "life span." Generally, it can accommodate children from 1 to 8 years of age, which would make it the last seat your child ever needs.

Disadvantages

This booster seat type can present a couple of disadvantages:

+ Narrower harness straps – Its harness straps may be noticeably narrower than the straps on a forward-facing or convertible seat. Narrower straps are more prone to getting twisted and therefore may complicate buckling a child in properly. In addition, they provide less surface area to absorb impact forces in a crash.

High-Back Booster Seat Without Harness

+ Arm rests – Some models feature arm rests that can make it harder to fasten the seat belt when using the booster in the belt-positioning mode.

Characteristics	Forward-Facing Car Seats		
	Convertible Seat	Forward-Facing Seat	High-Back Belt-Positioning Booster Seat
Age range for use	0-4 years	1-4 years	1-8 years
Rear-facing ability	yes	no	no
5-point harness available	yes	yes	yes
Wide straps	yes	yes	check make & model

For optimal protection, children should remain in a booster seat until they're at least 8 years old, unless they've reached the height of 4 feet 9 inches.

FORWARD-FACING RECOMMENDATION

Safety wise, your best initial option for a forward-facing seat is a convertible seat, which allows your child to remain rear facing (the safer position) longer because of its higher rear-facing weight maximum. Once she reaches the convertible seat's rear-facing weight limit, she can ride forward facing in it until she's approximately 4 years old. Then it's time to switch her to a belt-positioning booster seat, which she can ride in until she's 8 years old or 4 feet 9 inches tall.

For help in selecting a forward-facing car seat, you can consult the NHTSA's Car Seat Ease of Use Ratings for Forward-Facing Seats, which is available at the NHTSA website. Please see Appendix D for guidance on locating this and other helpful online child safety resources.

Recommended Car Seat Sequence

If your budget will permit it, we recommend that you purchase the following sequence of car seats:

1. **Infant-only seat with base**, which your child can remain in until she reaches its rear-facing weight limit (20 – 22 pounds).

2. **Convertible seat**, which your child can ride in rear facing until she reaches the rear-facing weight limit (which is higher than the infant-only seat's rear-facing weight limit); and then forward facing until she reaches 40 pounds.

3. **Belt-positioning booster seat**, which your child can ride in from 40 pounds (which she'll reach around 4 years of age) until she's 8 years old or 4 feet 9 inches tall.

▷ REVIEW OF KEY SAFETY POINTS ◁

Let's summarize the key points covered in this chapter:

✔ Different car seat types are designed to protect children at different ages/developmental stages.

✔ Car seats are rear facing or forward facing.

Infant-Only Seats

✔ Designed for babies up to approximately 1 year of age.

✔ Children older than 1 year should continue to ride in an infant-only seat so long as they weigh less than the seat's mandated weight limit (20 – 22 pounds).

✔ 2 options:

- Without a base

- With a base

✔ Advantages, with or without a base:

- Convenience of carrier feature

- Smaller seat shell permits better fit (eliminates need for added head support)

✔ Advantages, with a base

- Easy "snap on" installation

- Adjustable base permits proper seat positioning without need for a towel or foam insert

- Most convenient model for placement in middle position in back seat

✔ Disadvantage – A child could outgrow the seat before she turns 1 year old, compelling parents to have to get a convertible seat before her first birthday.

Convertible Seats

✔ Generally for children from birth until they reach 40 pounds (around 4 years old).

✔ Children ride rear facing until they are older than 1 year and have reached the seat's rear-facing weight limit.

✔ Advantages:

- Versatility (rear or forward facing) makes it cost-effective because it's good for 4 years

- Wider harness straps resist twisting and provide more surface area to absorb crash impact forces

✔ Disadvantages:

- Bigger seat shell means a newborn might require added head support

- Lacks the convenient portability of an infant-only seat, which can be used as an infant carrier

Forward-Facing Seats

✔ Designed for children who weigh from 20 to 40 pounds.

✔ 3 harness types available:

1. 5-point harness

2. T-shield harness

3. Tray-shield harness

✔ Advantages:

- Harness strap versatility

- Wider straps resist twisting and provide more surface area to absorb crash impact forces

Booster Seats

✔ Boosts child to height that makes it safe to use vehicle's seat belt to restrain her.

✔ 2 types:

- No-back belt-positioning booster seat

- High-back belt-positioning booster seat

✔ For optimal protection, children should remain in boosters until they're 8 years old or 4 feet 9 inches tall.

High-Back Belt-Positioning Booster Seats

✔ Offers versatility – can serve as either a forward-facing toddler seat or booster seat.

✔ Comes with a 5-point harness, which is used to restrain children when they weigh from 20 to 40 pounds.

✔ The seat is converted to a belt-positioning booster seat once a child reaches 40 pounds (around age 4).

✔ Advantage – An economical choice for parents because it can accommodate children from 1 to 8 years old.

✔ Disadvantages:

- Narrower harness straps

- Arm rests on some models can make it harder to fasten the
  seat belt in the belt-positioning mode

Recommendations

✔ Rear-facing seat: infant only with base.

✔ Forward-facing seat: convertible.

✔ Sequence of seats:

1. Infant only with base

2. Convertible

3. Belt-positioning booster

Now that we've completed our overview of your car seat options, let's
undertake a discussion of how to correctly install and properly use
your child's car seat.

CHAPTER 9

Car Seat Installation and Use

A car seat is your child's number one protector out on the road. Studies show that car seats reduce child fatalities in auto accidents by over 70%, depending on the child's age and the positioning of the seat. However, these dramatic results are achieved only when seats are installed correctly and children are buckled in properly.

Unfortunately, improper installation and use is alarmingly common in the United States. How widespread is the problem? According to the US Department of Transportation (DOT), as many as 4 out of 5 car seats are installed and/or used incorrectly. Which means that the great majority of young children who ride in car seats are at increased risk of serious injury or death. In greatest jeopardy are the nearly 12% of children who the DOT estimates ride entirely unrestrained in vehicles.

Here's the bottom line on car seats: You can buy the most expensive model with the top safety rating. But that seat won't provide the full protection it was designed to provide unless 1) it is installed correctly, according to the manufacturer's instructions; and 2) your child is buckled in properly.

Let's address the main safety considerations with installation and use.

PROPER INSTALLATION

When parents install their car seats incorrectly, they end up jeopardizing their children's safety. There are few things you'll do that matter more to your child's well-being in his first years than installing his car seat properly.

Of course, if installing a seat were easy, we'd all get it right, no problem. But it's not easy. The difficulty it poses goes a long way toward explaining why a majority of seats are not installed correctly. What's the surest way to get it right? Get some help.

Help's at Hand: Certified Installers

Fortunately, there is a nationwide resource available to assist you with installation. This resource is called a certified car seat technician. These technicians undergo intensive training to be able to install all makes and models of car seats in every kind of personal vehicle. And to maintain their certification, they must stay current with the latest car seat design modifications and installation standards.

Such a technician not only will expertly install your child's car seat. He or she also will answer any questions you might have, and can show you how to do it correctly should you need to reinstall the seat in the future.

You can locate a local car seat technician in either of 2 ways:

Via the Internet

Appendix D offers direction on locating websites with listings of certified technicians nationwide. The National Highway Traffic Safety Administration (NHTSA) has an online directory of technicians, compiled from data provided to it by the Automobile Association of America (AAA).

By Telephone

If you don't have Internet access, you can locate a car seat technician by calling the DOT Auto Safety Hotline at (888) 327-4236. You also can contact your local police or fire department to see if either has certified technicians among its ranks. In addition, the maternity ward at a local hospital should be able to refer you to a certified installer in your area.

There is usually no charge for this service, which generally is offered as part of public safety initiatives.

Position, Placement, and Attachment

Properly installing your child's car seat involves 3 factors: 1) seat position (rear or forward facing); 2) seat placement (back seat, side or middle); and 3) seat attachment to the vehicle. Each must be right for your little passenger to reap the maximum safety benefit.

Position and Placement

All car seats for children under age 1 and less than 20 pounds should be rear facing and located in the back seat of the vehicle. We know from Chapter 8 that rear-facing seats include *infant-only seats* (with or without a base) and *convertible seats* in the rear-facing position. A rear-facing seat is mandated for infancy because it provides the greatest head, neck, and back support to a baby in case of a crash or sudden

Safety Note

Air Bag Warning

You should never install a rear-facing car seat in the front seat of a vehicle with air bags. These safety devices have saved many, many teen and adult lives. But for a baby in a rear-facing seat, an air bag is a deadly hazard if it deploys in a collision. The seat simply can't withstand the tremendous force of impact from the air bag. In such a situation, a baby would have little chance of surviving the impact.

stop. We'd all be safer if we rode facing rearward in our cars – drivers excluded, of course!

The rear-facing seat should always be placed in the vehicle's back seat, to best protect your baby in the event of a head-on collision, which happens to be the most common type of auto collision. Studies show that passengers, regardless of age, are 25% more likely to survive a head-on crash if they're located in the back seat.

Moreover, you should consider placing the car seat in the middle of your vehicle's back seat, for better protection in case of a side collision. You'll probably find that an infant-only seat with base is easiest to manage in the middle because all you have to do, once the base is installed, is snap the seat (with your baby already buckled in it) into the base. Middle seat placement with a convertible seat in the rear-facing position will likely be more challenging. Or it just might not be possible if you have to fit a couple of car seats in the back seat.

Car seats for children who exceed rear-facing weight limits should, of course, be forward facing. Forward-facing seats, like rear-facing seats, should always be in the vehicle's back seat, and when possible, positioned in the middle.

Let's cover one other point before we get to seat attachment to your vehicle. As you might recall from Chapter 8, an infant-only seat has a handle for when it's used as a carrier. This adjustable handle has 2 settings – *up*, for carrying outside the car; and *down*, for travel in the car. If you own an infant-only seat, make sure you always lower the handle to the down position when your baby's strapped in it and you're about to go for a drive. The handle in the up position could endanger your infant in the event of an accident.

Attachment to Vehicle

Installing your child's car seat correctly in your vehicle might drive you bonkers...and put you in traction! Most parents have stories of how maddeningly complicated and difficult it can be. Proof of how difficult is the fact, as we noted previously, that an estimated 80% of seats are installed incorrectly. The challenge of doing it right is why we recommend that you spare yourself the frustration and have a certified car seat technician install your child's seat. But if you're determined to do it yourself, you need to be aware of the 2 systems for attaching a car seat to the vehicle seat.

The 2 installation systems

There are 2 basic systems for attaching a car seat to the vehicle seat: 1) seat belt installation; and 2) LATCH installation.

One system is as safe as the other, when implemented properly. Therefore, you should use whichever system is easiest with your child's particular car seat.

Seat belt installation

With this system, you use your vehicle's seat belt restraint to fasten the safety seat to the vehicle's back seat. Be sure to follow the car seat manufacturer's instructions carefully. Consult your vehicle' owner's manual, too, for guidance on installation with the seat belt. Don't improvise or skip steps. You might need to read the instructions a few times, confusing as they can be. And if you're really struggling to get it right, remember 4 words – certified car seat technician!

A convertible seat has 2 different belt paths through which to run the vehicle's seat belt restraint – 1 for rear-facing position and 1 for forward-facing position. If you have a convertible seat, therefore, you need to be sure you're using the correct path, depending on the position in which you're installing the seat.

If you're installing a forward-facing seat, or a convertible seat in the forward-facing position, be sure to route the seat belt *between* the seat's shell and harness adjustment straps. You won't be able to adjust the harness straps if you place the seat belt over them. The final installation step with any forward-facing seat is to put your knee on the seat, exert as much downward pressure as you can, and pull the seat belt tight, thereby immobilizing the seat as much as possible.

You can further stabilize a forward-facing seat by securing it with a tether, which fastens to the seat back and must be attached to an anchor point in your vehicle. We'll describe how this works shortly, under "Using a tether"; but first, let's cover the second installation system, which is all about anchors and tethers.

LATCH installation

LATCH stands for **L**ower **A**nchors and **T**ethers for **CH**ildren. This newer system promotes safety by standardizing and simplifying installation – regardless of which car seat or vehicle you happen to own. LATCH is an alternative to using the seat belt system in newer vehicles. All vehicles and child safety seats manufactured since September 1, 2002, are LATCH ready.

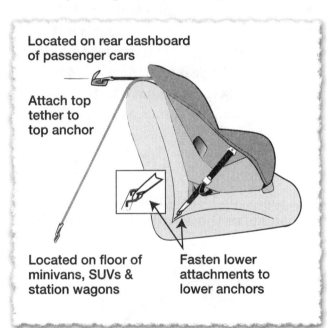

Located on rear dashboard of passenger cars

Attach top tether to top anchor

Located on floor of minivans, SUVs & station wagons

Fasten lower attachments to lower anchors

With the LATCH system, cars, minivans, SUVs and light trucks must have anchor points between the vehicle's seat cushion and the seat back in at least 2 rear seating positions. They also must have tether anchors. Child safety seats have to have a lower set of attachments that fasten to the vehicle anchors. Most types of forward-facing seats also have a top strap (or tether) that attaches to the anchors in the vehicle. You won't use this top tether with most models of rear-facing seats.

LATCH won't be an option for you if either your vehicle or car seat was manufactured before September 1, 2002. But if it is an option, be sure to carefully follow the LATCH installation instructions provided in your car seat and vehicle owner's manuals.

Whether you use LATCH or the seat belt system, your last step is to test the seat to make sure it's installed satisfactorily before you let your child ride in it. The seat should not move more than 1 inch forward or sideways when you push or tug on it. If it does, it's too loose.

Also, no matter which system you use, a rear-facing seat should be reclined at a 45 degree angle from upright. What if the seat is not at a 45-degree angle when you're done installing it? Unfasten it and insert a rolled towel or foam noodle beneath the seat to achieve the 45-degree angle. You might be spared this step if you have an infant-only seat with a base because the base unit usually comes with a knob that adjusts the seat angle.

Using a tether

A tether is an adjustable strap that's used to anchor the car seat, further stabilizing it. Expecting parents or those with an infant might not be familiar with tethers because they're used almost exclusively with car seats in the forward-facing position.

A tether has hook fasteners at either end. These hooks are used to attach the tether at one end to the car seat's upper back; and at the other end to the tether anchor point,

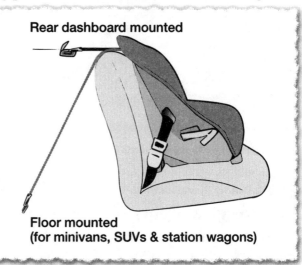

Rear dashboard mounted

Floor mounted
(for minivans, SUVs & station wagons)

either on the vehicle's rear dashboard or floor. Most passenger vehicles have an anchor point mounted on the rear dash area. The anchor points in SUVs, minivans, and station wagons are located on the floor or on the vehicle's seat back.

A top tether strap further reduces the injury risk by restricting the car seat's range of movement – and hence that of the child's head and neck – in a forward crash. Whether or not you use a top tether, you still need to attach your child's car seat to your vehicle, in accordance with the manufacturer's instructions and your vehicle's owner's manual. All new cars, minivans, SUVs and light trucks manufactured since September 2000 come equipped with a tether anchor. If you're driving a vehicle made before September 2000, you can contact your dealer about having one installed.

You'll probably be happy to know that we've finished our introduction to correct car seat installation! Now we're ready to cover how to properly secure your child in his seat. But before we do, let's digress. Let's first outline what's involved in switching a convertible seat to the forward-facing position, as parents must do when their children reach the seat's rear-facing weight limit.

Steps to Switch a Convertible Seat to Forward Facing

You need to take the following few steps to change your child's convertible seat from the rear-facing to forward-facing position. Be sure to consult the manufacturer's instructions for details on each of these.

1. **Change seat setting** – The first step in changing direction is to switch the seat setting to forward facing. The forward-facing setting places the seat in a more upright position than when it was rear facing. A seat back positioned closer to vertical is safest for a child when facing forward.

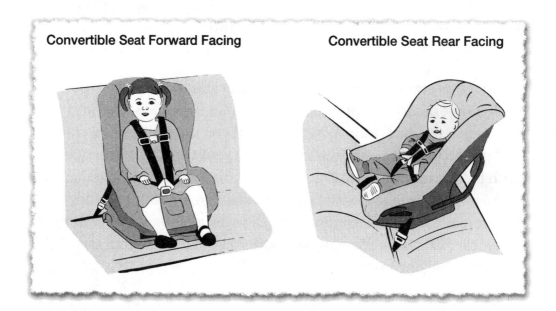

Convertible Seat Forward Facing   Convertible Seat Rear Facing

2. Change seat belt routing – If you're using the seat belt restraint to attach the convertible seat to your vehicle, you must change the path of the seat belt. You need to route the seat belt through the path designated for the forward-facing position.

3. Reposition harness straps – When switching the seat to forward facing, you must move the shoulder straps to the top set of positioning slots, which are reinforced. All the convertible seat's lower positioning slots are designed for the rear-facing position only.

For extra stability in the forward-facing position, you should secure the seat with a top tether, as we described previously under "Using a tether."

When to Change Direction: From Rear Facing to Forward Facing

The time will come when you must switch your growing child from a rear- to forward-facing car seat. That time won't be before his first birthday. Children must be rear facing until they're at least 1 year old *and* weigh 20 pounds. The many makes and models of seats suitable for infants have different weight maximums for safe use. Therefore, you need to find out the specifications for your child's car seat to determine when it's time to change direction. (Please see the Car Seat Log in Appendix C. You can use this handy tool to catalog the vital statistics for your car seat.) For infant-only seat owners, the change will mean getting a convertible or forward-facing seat. For convertible seat owners, it will mean converting to the forward-facing position.

Here are the when-to-change-direction guidelines for both seat types:

Infant-only seat

You must stop using an infant-only seat when your child reaches its weight limit, which generally is 20 to 22 pounds, depending on the specific seat model. What if your child reaches the weight limit before turning 1 year old? Your only option is to put him in a convertible seat, rear facing.

Convertible seat

You may shift a convertible seat from rear to forward facing when your child is at least 1 year old *and* weighs 20 pounds. It's far safer, however, to keep your child facing back until he reaches the seat's rear-facing weight limit.

Safety Note

When to Change Convertible Seats to Forward Facing

According to the NHTSA and convertible seat manufacturers, a child should be kept rear facing until at least 1 year of age <u>and</u> 20 pounds. But many parents seem to be in a rush to switch their car seat to the forward-facing position. Maybe it's because they're so eager to finally see that darling face looking back at them in the rear-view mirror.

They might not be in such a hurry if they realized that it's actually much safer to keep a child rear facing as long as possible. Experience shows that a baby is much better protected in the rear-facing than the forward-facing position because his head and neck receive much more support in the event of a crash. Some convertible seats have rear-facing weight limits up to 32 pounds. These seats permit a child to be rear facing until at least 2 years of age.

If you have a convertible seat, be in no rush to switch your child to the forward-facing position. For safety's sake, keep him rear facing as long as possible.

SECURING YOUR CHILD IN THE SEAT

You've installed the safety seat in your vehicle and tested it. Now you're ready to secure your child in the seat. Doing so the right way is just as important to protecting your little one as installing the seat correctly. And safety demands that you do it properly every time, regardless of how rushed or tired you are, or how uncooperative your child may be. Getting your child properly secured in his seat from the outset is habit forming. And this good habit on your part will make him safer for all the years he must ride in a car seat.

Let's cover the 3 factors you need to be attentive to in securing your child in the seat:

+ Harness straps

+ Buckling sequence

+ Extra cushioning (with newborns)

Harness Straps

There are 3 keys to proper harness strap use: 1) positioning; 2) strap tension; and 3) avoiding bulky clothing.

Positioning

Your infant-only or convertible seat has adjustment slots built into the seat padding and shell. The harness straps should be threaded through the slots at or below your baby's shoulders for all seats in

Safety Note

A Frustrating "Twist"

Harness straps tend to get twisted. This is particularly true with infant-only seats and some models of booster seats with a 5-point harness. These seats generally have narrower straps than convertible seats do. You may find it helpful to keep the harness system on your child's seat buckled and snug when not in use to prevent the straps from twisting. If they do become twisted, you might have to remove, straighten and re-thread them. Keep in mind that you should never buckle your little one in his seat if the straps are twisted.

the rear-facing position. For a newborn, use the lowest harness slot position. You then can adjust the straps to the higher slots as your baby grows. But remember – the straps should always be at or below your baby's shoulder level for as long as the seat is rear facing.

For a convertible seat in the forward-facing position, harness straps should go through the top set of slots. Also, the straps should be positioned at or above a child's shoulder level for all forward-facing seats.

Strap tension

The harness straps should be buckled snugly around your infant or toddler. Adjust the tension so you can slip only 1 finger beneath the straps at your child's chest.

Bulky clothing

For optimal safety, harness straps must be a snug fit over shoulders and between legs. Bulky clothing can frustrate your efforts to get such a fit. It's best to dress your child in outfits that keep his legs free. If you want to cover him up, buckle the harness around him first, and then place a blanket over him (but only up to chest level). Bulky clothing – a snow suit or winter jacket, for example – could lead you to loosen the harness too much.

Forward-facing fact: the importance of harness straps

Children riding in a rear-facing seat enjoy the safety benefit of the seat's shell, which provides added protection to the head, neck and back in a collision. Forward-facing seats, unfortunately, don't confer this same benefit. What protects children seated forward facing in the event of an accident are the harness straps. Therefore, it is *extra* imperative to secure your child properly with the harness straps in a forward-facing seat. You must take care to do it right every time you buckle him in – no matter how rushed or tired you are; and regardless of how uncooperative he may be. Always position the straps at or above his shoulder level and adjust them until they're snug. And never buckle him up if the straps are twisted. If need be, remove twisted straps, straighten them, and then re-thread them.

Buckling Sequence

Follow these 5 steps to secure your child properly in his seat:

1. Place him in the seat

2. Buckle the harness at the crotch

3. Tighten the harness straps as already described

4. Buckle the chest clip at armpit level

5. Inspect for proper fit

Get in the habit of following this sequence. Many parents attach the chest clip first, which may interfere with adjusting the harness straps and lead to a poor – and therefore unsafe – fit. If your child tends to squirm when placed in the seat, you might have to attach the chest clip first. If so, you need to undo the chest clip after buckling the crotch strap and then complete the proper buckling sequence.

Extra Cushioning

At first, your newborn's car seat might be too roomy to support his head properly. If so, his head could flop around because his neck isn't yet strong enough to hold it up. You can remedy this problem by filling the empty space in the seat shell with extra cushioning. The simplest solution is to roll up a small towel or blanket and tuck it around your baby's shoulders and head. But make sure you don't accidentally cover his nose or mouth with this added padding. Also, you should never place any thick padding or cushioning beneath or behind your baby in the car seat.

BOOSTER SEATS

At 40 pounds, your child will graduate to a belt-positioning booster seat, at which point you'll restrain him not with a harness but with your vehicle's seat belt. Here are a few key guidelines you need to follow to ensure that you secure him properly in the booster:

+ Always use both the lap and shoulder belt to restrain him; the lap belt alone won't provide sufficient protection.

◆ Never place the shoulder belt behind your child's back or under his arm; doing so could put him at risk of very serious, or even fatal, injury in the event of a crash.

◆ Make sure the shoulder belt crosses his chest and rests snugly on the shoulder.

◆ Make sure the lap belt rests low across the pelvis or hip area – never across the stomach area.

Also, be attentive to your child's height in the seat. If his ears are higher than either the back of the booster seat or your vehicle's seat back cushion, then he's too tall for the booster.

REVIEW OF KEY SAFETY POINTS

Let's summarize the key points covered in this chapter:

✔ Car seats dramatically reduce child fatalities when installed and used correctly.

✔ As many as 4 out of 5 car seats are installed and/or used incorrectly.

Proper Installation

✔ A car seat won't provide full protection unless it's installed correctly and the child is buckled in properly.

✔ The way to be certain your child's car seat is installed correctly is to have a certified car seat technician do it.

✔ Both rear- and forward-facing seats should be put in the vehicle's back seat and, when possible, positioned in the middle.

✔ Never install a rear-facing car seat in the front seat of a vehicle with air bags.

✔ 2 systems for car seat installation:

  - Seat belt system

  - LATCH system

✔ A properly installed seat shouldn't move more than 1 inch forward or sideways when you push or tug on it.

✔ A top tether strap reduces the child injury risk by restricting the car seat's range of movement in a forward crash.

✔ Children must ride rear facing until at least 1 year old *and* 20 pounds.

✔ It's safest to keep a child in the rear-facing position for as long as possible (i.e., until the child reaches the seat's rear-facing weight limit).

Proper Use

✔ Make sure you buckle your child in his seat properly every time.

✔ Harness straps should always be positioned at or below your baby's shoulders for as long as he rides rear facing.

✔ Harness straps should always be positioned at or above your child's shoulders for all forward-facing seats.

✔ Harness straps should be a snug fit against your child – i.e., you should only be able to slip 1 finger beneath the straps at the level of the chest clip.

✔ Proper 5-step buckling sequence:

    1. Place child in the seat

    2. Buckle harness at the crotch

    3. Tighten harness straps

    4. Buckle chest clip at armpit level

    5. Inspect for proper fit

✔ If a car seat shell is too roomy to support a newborn's head properly, fill in the space with extra cushioning (e.g., a small rolled-up towel).

Booster Seats

✔ Always use both the vehicle's lap and shoulder belts to buckle your child in a belt-positioning booster seat.

✔ Never place the shoulder belt behind your child's back or under his arm.

✔ The shoulder belt should cross your child's chest and rest snugly on his shoulder.

✔ The lap belt should rest low across the pelvis or hip area – not across the stomach.

This concludes our look at how to properly install and use car seats – which means we've completed our overview of car seat safety. Next, let's turn to common household hazards that threaten young children. We begin with choking hazards.

CHAPTER

10

Choking Hazards

A grape. A coin. Hard candy. A magic marker cap. Essentially harmless objects in the hands of adults or older children. But in the hands of infants or toddlers – or *mouths*, more specifically – these items become serious choking hazards.

Any one of us, regardless of age, could choke if we swallowed something too big around and it stuck in our throat, blocking the air way. But the risk of choking is by far greatest for children under 5 years of age. No surprise in this. Infants and toddlers have narrow air ways. They're only just learning how to eat solids (and finding out it's not as easy as it looks). And they don't understand the choking danger. They simply lack the judgment to recognize that there's a threat. So they tend to put in their mouths whatever they're able to get their hands on. From tiny hand to tiny mouth – it's a very natural part of discovery for babies and tots who are trying to figure out the world around them.

This fact of life with young children means that you, as a parent, must be constantly alert to choking dangers. And you need to raise your alertness level once your baby is crawling and eating table food, which will happen at around 9 months old. Your most reliable ally against choking is, of course, prevention. Effective prevention requires aware-ness ("What food and nonfood items is my child vulnerable to chok-ing on?"), precaution ("Did I slice the grape in quarters? Did I store the balloons well out of reach?"), and attentive supervision ("What did my tot just find beneath the sofa?").

Our aim in this chapter is to familiarize you with choking hazards for children under age 5. Let's begin with a few statistics that convey the nature and scope of the danger. Then we'll identify the more common choking hazards and outline what you can do to protect your child from them.

▷ THE NUMBERS ON CHOKING ◁

What do the numbers on children choking tell us? Consider these sta-tistics from the US Centers for Disease Control and Prevention (CDC):

- ✦ In 2000, among children under age 15, there were 160 fatal choking episodes caused by food or other items (mainly toys or small household items).

- ✦ Nearly 60% of these choking deaths were caused by toys or household items that the victims swallowed.

- ✦ Most choking fatalities are among children under 5 years of age.

- ✦ For every choking fatality, there are more than 100 nonfatal episodes treated in hospital ERs every year.

- ✦ Upwards of 60% of nonfatal choking episodes with children involve food items.

As the numbers show, food and nonfood items alike pose hazards to young children. Therefore, you need to be wise to both edible and inedible choking dangers that could threaten your little one. Which means you must be alert to choking hazards during meal/snack time *and* play time.

► MEAL TIME AND SNACK TIME ◄

As babies grow and become toddlers, they're learning how to chew and swallow, which can make for quite an adventure at meal or snack time. During this developmental stage, children tend to not chew food thoroughly; to swallow food whole; or to bite off more than they can chew – *literally*. So, they are at higher risk of having food become stuck in their throat and choking.

It's your job to protect your child from this danger, through prevention. Start with the most basic precaution: Don't give your little one any food item she might struggle with. Most of the time, common sense is a reliable guide to what she can or cannot handle, given her age and demonstrated progress with solid food. But not always. For further guidance, consult with your pediatrician at your child's wellness visits about safe foods for whatever age she's reached.

Another important precaution is to always chop up any firm, round food into manageable pieces before serving it. (For infants and tots, this means no bigger than 1/2 inch in diameter.) Doing so greatly reduces the choking risk for children under 4 years old, for whom firm and round food items can be a deadly danger. Be mindful of the following common choking hazards, which should be properly sized and shaped to make them safer for consumption:

+ Hot dogs – Always cut length-wise and then into small pieces

+ Meat or cheese chunks

+ Whole grapes – Always cut into quarter pieces

+ Raw vegetables – Always cut into small, non-round strips or pieces

Also be alert to the well-established choking risk with the following other foods:

* Nuts and seeds
* Peanut butter
* Popcorn
* Raisins

Once you've served your child a meal or snack with no obvious choking hazard, you face the next safety must: Make her sit down while she eats. That means either strapped in a highchair, or at a table with her fanny in a chair. Children who "eat on the move" or while playing around are more susceptible to a choking mishap. All it takes is for an infant or toddler with a mouthful of food to stumble or trip. The best precaution against this happening is to always keep snack or meal time separate from play time in your household. As a rule, don't let your child walk, run, play, or lie down with food in her mouth.

Even when you have your little one sitting down with her food, you need to keep a watchful eye on her while she noshes. In choking episodes, trouble usually strikes when a parent isn't looking or paying close attention. You also need to instruct your child – again and again and again, until she proves she's getting the message (which might not be until her teens) – to eat slowly, take one bite at a time, and chew thoroughly before swallowing.

Let's cover one more point before moving on to choking hazards during play time. Tempted as you might be to give your baby or tot a snack in the car when you're out driving, you really shouldn't. It's too risky. Just consider: If you had to jam on the brakes without warning, your child could swallow in the wrong way and end up with her snack lodged in her air way. What's more, if your little one did have a choking episode, you would be in no position, behind the wheel of a moving car, to come to her immediate aid.

Safety Note

Candy Hazard

Experience warns us that candy is a big culprit in choking episodes with children under age 5. According to the CDC, candy is responsible for 25% of choking-related visits to hospital ERs by children ages 1 to 4.

There are a couple kinds of candy, broadly speaking, to be wary of:

- ✦ Hard — Hard candies (e.g., sour balls, jaw breakers, restaurant mints) pose the greatest danger, accounting for 65% of early childhood choking incidents treated in ERs. These candies can so easily slip down the throat of a little person and get stuck.

- ✦ Chewy or gooey — Anything chewy or gooey (e.g., caramels, taffy, gummy bears, fruit chews) is a danger to plug up the throat of an infant or toddler when swallowed.

Chewing gum, too, is hazardous because it can easily slide from a young child's mouth to throat and become lodged. Given these risks, it's probably best not to give your baby any candy at all in her first year. When you do start letting her have it, use your best judgment as to what she can handle. There's no need to rush her introduction to the hard or chewy stuff. For the time being, give yourself — and her baby teeth — a break.

▷ PLAY TIME ◁

As we've already pointed out, young children are about as likely to choke on something inedible, such as a small toy or household item, as on food. And statistics tell us that these nonfood items actually pose the deadliest danger to those under age 5. Young children are likeliest to get their hands on such items when they're playing. Your mission, therefore, is to make sure your baby's or toddler's play environment is clear of any toys or other objects that could endanger her if they ended up in her mouth.

> What, in particular, should you look out for? The following are some of the nonfood items that infants and toddlers most commonly choke on:
>
> + Latex balloons
>
> + Small balls
>
> + Marbles
>
> + Toys with small parts
>
> + Toys that can be compressed to fit entirely into a child's mouth
>
> + Coins
>
> + Pen or marker caps
>
> + Small button-type batteries
>
> + Medicine syringes

We'll have more to say about a few of these shortly. But before we do, let's outline some general precautions you should take to protect your child from the choking danger that nonfood items pose:

✦ Keep your small household items (e.g., keys, loose change, hardware, sewing kit stuff) in a secure place, either locked away or somewhere dependably out of reach.

✦ Always scan your baby's immediate environment for possible hazards (a stray button, a penny, a bolt, small jewelry). Small objects just have an uncanny knack for ending up where curious little hands can find them.

✦ Once your baby's crawling, make it a regular habit to check for possible choking hazards on floors, under furniture, and between chair and sofa cushions.

✦ If you have older children, be attentive to what they're doing around your infant or toddler. Often, choking episodes happen when an older brother or sister hands a dangerous toy or other small object to a baby sibling. It takes only a brief lapse in your supervision for such a hazardous hand-off to take place.

Just how concerned need you be about your child putting something hazardous in her mouth as she's moving through her toddler years? In part, let her demonstrated behavior be your guide. Some tots put any and everything they can get their hands on in their mouths, even when they've been warned repeatedly not to. Others show much less inclination to do so. It comes down to knowing your child and what she's likely to do, based on watching her over time. But be careful. Past behavior goes only so far in predicting what might happen next. Any toddler, at any given moment, is a candidate to slip something dangerous between her lips. So you can't ever afford to get lax about supervision.

Coins

Coins are such a common choking hazard that they deserve special mention here. According to the CDC, nearly 20% of choking-related visits to hospital ERs by 1- to 4-year-olds involve coins. It's the rare older infant or toddler who doesn't find pennies, nickels, dimes, and quarters irresistible. And generally what's the first thing a young child does if she gets her mitts on a coin? Puts it in her mouth. The fact is that a coin's size and shape make it a sure bet to get stuck in the throat if swallowed. Given this danger, parents mustn't let an infant or tot handle coins. Make sure your loose change isn't anywhere your child could get to it. And look on the bright side – soon enough your little one won't have any interest in your pocket change. As she gets a little older her fixation will shift, rather, to the green paper in your wallet. At which point you'll have a whole other problem on your hands!

Toys

Toys should be fun for children and benefit them developmentally. Unfortunately, certain toys in some circumstances can pose a choking hazard to the infants or toddlers who play with them. We know that the choking danger is greatest for children under 3 years of age. The vulnerability of this age group undoubtedly explains why strict manufacturing guidelines exist for the size of products sold for children under age 3. These guidelines are as follows:

+ Products generally must be greater than 1.25 (or 1$1/4$) inches in diameter.

+ Pacifiers must be greater than 1.68 (or approximately 1$2/3$) inches in diameter.

+ Small balls must be greater than 1.75 (or 1$3/4$) inches in diameter.

To help protect your child from choking dangers during play time, confirm that toys are a safe size. (See the Safety Note "Measuring for Safety" for a handy measuring tip.) You should also take the following precautions:

+ Heed the recommended age minimum for toys. If it says "for ages 3 years and up" on the box, don't let your 2-year-old play with it. In terms of product safety, toys are designed with a child's age – and therefore level of physical and mental development – in mind. So a toy with small parts that's safe for a 5-year-old might be a choking danger to a 2-year-old. Precocious as your little one may be, it's just not a good idea to let her play with toys graded for children older than her. Always follow the recommended age guidelines for toys.

✦ Keep older children's toys out of reach. This is another way of stating our point about age appropriateness. If you have older kids, you mustn't let your little one play with their toys, much as she'll want to. Teach the older children to always put away

Safety Note

Measuring for Safety

Any object with a diameter less than 13/4 inches can be a choking hazard for young children, especially those under 3 years of age. This choking danger, determined as it is by size, is responsible for the manufacturing guidelines that require products marketed for children under age 3 to be certain minimum diameters.

Short of toting around a tape measure, how can you quickly size up an object to tell if it's a choking hazard to your infant or toddler? Keep a cardboard tube from a standard roll of toilet paper or paper towels handy. The diameter of one of these tubes happens to be approximately 13/4 inches. So, as a rule of thumb, if an object fits through this cardboard roll, it will fit in an infant's or toddler's mouth and could get lodged in her throat.

their toys when play time's over so a baby brother or sister can't get to them.

A couple of toy items from our list of common nonfood hazards merit singling out because they pose such a serious choking threat:

1. **Balloons** – The Consumer Product Safety Commission (CPSC) ranks balloons among the leading choking hazards to children under 8 years of age. The danger is with un-inflated or busted balloons, which a young child can easily swallow and choke on. This usually happens in either of 2 ways:

+ A child unintentionally sucks an un-inflated balloon into her mouth while attempting to inflate it.

+ A child puts pieces of a broken balloon in her mouth and swallows them.

You can avoid this peril in your home by practicing balloon safety. First, make sure to store un-inflated balloons in a secure place, either locked up or well out of reach. Second, don't allow children under age 8 to play with un-inflated balloons. And third, when a balloon bursts, immediately collect and dispose of all the broken pieces before any can end up in a tiny mouth.

2. **Small balls** – Small balls, which abound in vending machines and kids' toys, are inviting targets for infants and toddlers. They're usually colorful. They roll when tossed or kicked. They don't look so different from certain kinds of candy. The problem, of course, is that young children's first impulse is to put such balls in their mouths. And any ball that fits in an infant's or toddler's mouth could end up lodging in her throat and blocking her air way. Given this danger, you should never let a child under age 4 play with a ball unless it's greater than 13/4 inches in diameter. If you also have older kids, it's a good idea to check regularly for any stray small balls that they might've wedged between the cushions of your upholstered furniture.

Safety Note

Bean Bag Chairs

During the 1990s, the CPSC recalled over 12 million zippered bean bag chairs because of the serious choking and suffocation hazard they pose to young children. A zipper permits access to the chair's foam pellet filling, which can suffocate or choke a child who inhales or swallows it. In some cases, toddlers have unzipped the chair cover and crawled inside, suffocating as a result. In others, children have choked while handling foam pellets that escaped through the zipper.

If you're in the market for a bean bag chair, be sure to buy a zipper-free model – or, at the least, one with a zipper that cannot be opened. Also make sure it's made of sturdy material that won't tear with normal use.

Vending Machines

Next time you walk into a department store or supermarket, take a closer look at the coin vending machines by the entrance or in the front foyer. You know – the ones that tempt your child to bug you for a dime or quarter so she can get what's inside. You'll see that the majority of them bear caution labels. These labels warn that the small balls and other mini toys dispensed by these machines can pose a choking hazard and thus aren't intended for children under 3 years of age.

⮞ LEARNING BASIC FIRST AID ⮜

In closing, let's raise one other important point: Taking all due precautions is no guarantee your child will never have a choking episode. Therefore, you should consider learning basic first aid skills, in the event you ever need to respond to an emergency situation with your child in your home. You can contact your local American Red Cross chapter or the American Heart Association to find out about training classes offered near you. These classes generally cover CPR and other first aid basics, including what to do for an infant or toddler who is choking.

⮞ REVIEW OF KEY SAFETY POINTS ⮜

Let's summarize the key points covered in this chapter:

- ✔ Children under age 5 are at higher risk of choking.

- ✔ Food, toys, and small household items all pose a choking hazard to infants and toddlers.

- ✔ The choking risk increases when a baby starts crawling and eating table food.

- ✔ Parents should consider learning basic first aid skills so they can respond immediately if their child is choking.

Meal or Snack Time

- ✔ Be alert to the following common food choking hazards:

  - Hot dogs

- Meat or cheese chunks

- Whole grapes

- Raw vegetables

- Nuts and seeds

- Popcorn

- Peanut butter

- Raisins

✔ Cut food for infants and toddlers into pieces no bigger than 1/2 inch in diameter.

✔ Don't permit your child to eat unless she's sitting down.

✔ Don't let your child walk, run, play, or lie down with food in her mouth.

✔ Always supervise your child during meal or snack time.

✔ Remind your child to eat slowly, take a bite at a time, and chew thoroughly before swallowing.

✔ Don't give your infant or toddler food in the car.

✔ Hard and chewy candy and chewing gum are serious choking hazards for children under age 5.

Play Time

✔ Be alert to the following common nonfood choking hazards:

- Latex balloons

- Small balls

- Marbles

- Toys with small parts

- Toys that can be compressed to fit entirely into a child's mouth

- Coins

- Pen or marker caps

- Small button-type batteries

- Medicine syringes

✔ Never permit your infant or toddler to play with coins.

✔ Keep small household items locked up or dependably out of reach.

✔ Once your baby's crawling, check regularly for possible hazards on floors, under furniture, and between chair and sofa cushions.

✔ Always supervise older children to make sure they don't hand a choking hazard to a baby sibling.

✔ Products marketed for children 3 years of age or younger must meet minimum size requirements to prevent choking:

- Products in general must be greater than 1.25 inches in diameter

- Pacifiers must be greater than 1.68 inches in diameter

- Small balls must be greater than 1.75 inches in diameter

✔ Always heed the manufacturer's recommended age minimum for toys.

✔ Practice balloon safety:

 - Don't let children younger than 8 years of age play with un-inflated balloons

 - Immediately collect and dispose of broken pieces when a balloon bursts

✔ Don't let your infant or toddler play with a ball unless it's greater than 13/4 inches in diameter.

We've concluded our overview of choking hazards. Next, let's consider what you can do to prevent accidental poison exposures in your home.

CHAPTER

11

$\mathcal{P}$oison $\mathcal{H}$azards

In 2002, US poison control centers fielded nearly 2.5 million calls about poison exposures. More than 90% of these poisonings happened in the home and involved such common household items as cleaning products, medicines, vitamins, cosmetics, and plants. Over half of the calls, moreover, involved children less than 6 years of age.

What these numbers clearly show is that accidental poisoning of young children in the home is common. Disturbingly so. And the risk of accidental exposure rises when babies start to crawl – and eventually to walk – and are getting into everything. Which means you need to become very alert to poison safety in your home. Protecting your child from poison exposure is, on one level, a fairly simple matter. All you need to do is 1) identify those things in your household which pose a poisoning risk, and 2) store them where your child cannot access them. Whenever you use any of these items, of course, you then must remember to return them to their safe storage once you're done.

What can make poison safety at home an on-going challenge is that the typically hazardous items are things we use all the time in the course of daily family life. And things we use so routinely we like to have quick and easy access to. So, if we're not careful, we can get lax about the preventive measures that keep our little ones from coming in contact with anything that could poison them.

In this chapter, we introduce you to some basic precautions you should take to prevent accidental poisonings in your home. We also outline steps to follow in the unfortunate event your child ever did swallow something poisonous, or that you suspected to be poisonous. Our first order of business is 1) to identify where in your household poison hazards are likely to be, and 2) to specify what these hazards include.

▶ WHERE ARE THE POISONS? ◀

Our homes aren't so different, one to the next, in terms of where we store things. This similarity means that we're likely to encounter the same poison hazards in the same locations in our homes. Here, then, are the rooms/areas where poison dangers tend to be located; and the hazards that we can expect to find in each:

- ✦ **Bedroom** – Cosmetics, colognes, hair spray, medications, mothballs

- ✦ **Bathroom** – Medicines, nail polish/nail polish remover, aerosol sprays, toilet cleaner, disinfectants, air fresheners, glass cleaner, abrasive cleanser

- ✦ **Laundry room** – Laundry detergent, bleach, spot/stain remover, pine oil, aerosol sprays

- **Kitchen** – Ant killer, metal polish (silver, copper or brass), dishwashing detergent, oven cleaner, drain clog remover, cigarettes

- **Garage** – Antifreeze, windshield cleaner, gasoline, charcoal lighter, termite killer, garden chemicals, fungicides, flea powder

- **Home workshop** – Solder, lead, cadmium, formaldehyde, solvents, paint thinner

Now that we've inventoried these common poison hazards – the *what* and the *where* – let's outline the few basic precautions you should follow to protect your child from the poisoning threat.

Basic Precautions

Prevention begins with storing all household chemical products and medicines out of your child's reach, out of sight, and preferably locked up. "Almost" counts in horseshoes, but not in poison prevention.

Here are some other precautions you should take:

- Always store household cleaning products and cosmetics in the containers they came in. The original container lists what toxic/hazardous agents are in a product. In the event of an accident, you'll need to be able to quickly identify what the product's contents are.

- Never use food or beverage containers to store household cleaning products or cosmetics. Storing a toxic liquid or powder in, say, a soda bottle or cracker tin invites a young child to think it's something to drink or eat.

✦ Read the label before using a household chemical product for the first time. Know what you're dealing with. A product might be an extreme poison hazard; if so, you might want to rethink using it or even having it in your home. (You're wisest, of course, to scrutinize a product label before making a purchase.)

✦ If you have a toddler, keep a close eye on him if you're using a toxic product with him in the vicinity. Never leave the product unattended – for example, while running to answer the phone. And always return it to safe storage, with cap or lid properly refastened, as soon as you're done with it. Half measures aren't good enough. "Not accessible" must mean just that – your child cannot get to the hazards.

One other thing, on the subject of general precautions: Be aware of the poison danger that household plants may pose. See our Safety Note for a discussion of this potential hazard.

WHAT IF A POISONING HAPPENS?

You've taken many precautions to avoid an accidental poisoning in your home. But somehow, despite your efforts, your child comes across something toxic and swallows it. What would you do? It's always best to be prepared in advance. Here are guidelines to follow in the event of such a mishap:

1. Try to stay calm. You can't help your child if you're in a panic. Take comfort in the fact that 3 out of 4 poison exposures are treated successfully in the victims' homes.

Safety Note

House Plants

Were you aware that many common household plants — such as holly, philodendron, mistletoe and elephant's ear, to name a few — are poisonous? A young child who ingests a hazardous indoor plant, therefore, can become very ill. To protect your child against this danger, you should identify all your indoor plants and then contact the Poison Control Center to determine if any of them are poisonous. Your home is no place for hazardous plants. Even nonpoisonous plants should be kept well out of an infant's or toddler's reach because their leaves or needles can be a choking hazard. And don't assume that a hanging plant is totally inaccessible to your baby. Keep in mind that its leaves might drop to the floor, where your little one could then reach them.

2. Try to determine how much of the substance your child ingested.

3. If your child seems to be in immediate danger (e.g., if he collapses or is having trouble breathing), call 911 for emergency assistance.

4. If your child is alert and responsive, call the National Poison Control Center at **1-800-222-1222**. If possible, have the following information ready when you call:

   ✦ Your child's age and estimated weight

+ The time at which the poison exposure happened

+ Details about the poisonous product, which are printed on its container/bottle (so have the container/bottle directly at hand)

5. Follow the instructions from the 911 operator or Poison Control Center.

It's also a good idea to stock your first aid kit with syrup of ipecac and activated charcoal, in case Poison Control tells you to give them to your child. But don't give them unless you've been instructed to do so.

POISON SAFETY CHECK

Bathroom. Kitchen. Garage or storage area. These are the locations in our homes where accidental poisonings happen most commonly. It's a good idea, therefore, to conduct a poison safety check in each of these areas in your household. The goal of such a screening is to identify any hazards and take steps to eliminate them.

We've organized a 3-part safety check for you in quiz format. The questions are meant to help you detect shortcomings and vulnerabilities in these 3 locations in your home. Your goal is to be able to answer "yes" to all the questions.

The Kitchen

We already identified the poisoning hazards most often found in kitchens under "Where Are the Poisons?" Consider the following questions about these items.

Safety Note

Tell-Tale Signs of Poison Exposure

You can't bank on your young child to tell you if he has ingested something poisonous — certainly not if he isn't speaking yet. Given the communication limits inherent with young children, you might have to rely on your own powers of observation to determine if your infant or toddler has been exposed to poison.

Here are some tell-tale signs to look out for:

+ Unusual stains or odors on clothing or skin

+ Unusual odor on the breath

+ Medicine or cleaning containers that are open or out of place

+ Physical symptoms such as drowsiness, stomach pain, sweating, drooling, or vomiting

+ Onset of fear or other sudden changes in behavior

Do harmful products have child-resistant caps? For optimal safety, household cleaners and other chemical products really should have child-resistant packaging to thwart young children, in case they ever somehow get their hands on these hazardous items.

Are dangerous products stored in their original containers?
They should be, for 2 reasons: 1) Labeling on the original
container specifies product contents and often outlines
first aid steps to take if the product is swallowed. 2) A
toxic/chemical product that's stored in a recycled beverage
or food container could encourage a littler person to
think it's something to drink or eat.

Are harmful products stored separately from food? They should be. Storing
anything that's hazardous if swallowed side by side with food or
beverages invites confusion. And confusion, in this case, could result
in accidental poisoning.

Are harmful products unreachable by young children? Rule one in poison
prevention is inaccessibility. It's best to store poison hazards up high,
and out of sight. In the kitchen, this means in elevated cabinets, or
maybe on upper closet shelves. Cabinets where known poison
dangers are stored should be locked; if need be, install child guards
on upper cabinets so a child who might somehow scale a counter top
can't open them.

 *Have you removed all hazards from beneath the sink?* Under the
kitchen sink is a very popular location for cleaning
products and supplies. The problem is that it's at ground
level, where older infants and toddlers roam. If you must
store hazards beneath the sink, install child guards on
the cabinet door to keep curious little people out.

The Bathroom

The precautions we recommended for securing poison hazards in
your kitchen are the same ones to follow with cleaning products and
cosmetics in your bathroom.

Let's focus here on poison safety with medicines, which most of us keep in the bathroom. Medicines are supposed to cure what ails us. But used improperly, they can do us harm. Like when we take more than we're supposed to. Or mix medications that shouldn't be taken together. Or take expired medicines. Infants and toddlers certainly are vulnerable to these medication dangers. Consider, for example, that every year numerous young children are poisoned by accidental aspirin overdoses. The harm medications can do to children under age 5 should lead all parents to check their bathrooms for looming hazards.

Do all aspirin and other drug bottles and containers have child-resistant caps? Aspirin, other over-the-counter medicines, and prescription drugs should come with child-resistant caps. Childproof packaging prevents accidents and can save lives. Make sure everything in your medicine chest has child-resistant closures (and that these are snapped on or screwed on properly). Get in the habit of checking your prescriptions at the time of purchase to make sure they're in child-resistant packaging.

Are all medicines in their original containers with the original labels? It's safe to say that you always want to be sure what you're giving your child in the way of medicine. And the surest way to avoid any uncertainty is to keep all medicines in their original containers. In some cases, prescription medicine labeling may not identify the drug or its ingredients. What then? Look for the prescription number on the original label. This number will enable the pharmacy where you filled the prescription to quickly identify the drug for you.

Have you disposed of all out-of-date prescriptions? When medicines age past a certain point, their chemical composition changes. Such change, with certain medications, can make them seriously unsafe for consumption. Given this potential danger, you don't want expired medicines lurking in your medicine cabinet. Go through all of your medications and check their dates. If you find any expired drugs, dispose of them immediately. The safest way to discard old drugs is to flush them down the toilet; at the same time, make sure to rinse the empty containers and throw them out.

Are all vitamins or mineral supplements in child-resistant packaging? They should be. Lots of vitamins and mineral supplements include contents that can be harmful if ingested by young children. Those with iron are particularly dangerous for children. Make sure any vitamins or mineral supplements stored in your bathroom (or anyplace else, for that matter) have child-resistant lids.

The Garage or Storage Area

The average garage or storage area is home to any number of deadly poison hazards. Items such as charcoal lighter, paint thinner and remover, antifreeze, turpentine, insecticides, and lawn chemicals. These all pose a grave threat to any child who might accidentally ingest them. So you need to make poison safety in your garage or storage area a top priority.

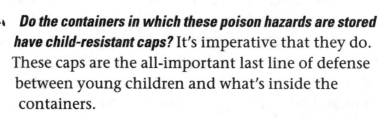

Do the containers in which these poison hazards are stored have child-resistant caps? It's imperative that they do. These caps are the all-important last line of defense between young children and what's inside the containers.

Are they stored in the original containers? By keeping such toxic substances in the original containers, you'll always be able to immediately identify what they are. Or put the reverse way, you'll never confuse what they are.

Do the containers still have the original labels on them? The original label lists a product's hazardous contents and usually includes important information regarding accidental poisoning with the product. You'll need this information if you have to call 911 or the Poison Control Center.

Have you made sure that no poisonous substances are stored in drinking glasses or beverage bottles? Storing toxic items in glasses or bottles could encourage a young child to think the contents are something drinkable.

Are all harmful products inaccessible to young children? Poison hazards should be out of sight, out of reach, and locked away.

How'd you make out? (Or should we say, how'd your bathroom, kitchen, and garage do?) For any "no" responses, you need to take measures to eliminate the detected poison hazards. These 3 household areas don't pass safety muster until all your answers are "yes."

Safety Note

National Poison Control Center

If your child ingests something poisonous but is still alert and responsive, call the National Poison Control Center at 1-800-222-1222. Keep this number posted right by your phone. The center is better equipped than your pediatrician to help you in this situation. And here's comforting news: In about 75% of poison exposure episodes, the victim can be treated successfully at home, without need for emergency medical care.

REVIEW OF KEY SAFETY POINTS

Let's summarize the key points covered in this chapter:

✔ The vast majority of accidental poisonings happen in the home and involve such common household items as cleaning products, cosmetics, and medicines.

✔ The majority of unintentional poisonings in the home involve children under 6 years of age.

✔ The accidental poisoning risk rises when babies start to crawl.

✔ Poison prevention involves 2 basic steps: 1) Identify all items in your home that pose a poison risk; and 2) Store these items where your child cannot get to them.

✔ Be alert to common household poison dangers and where they're usually located:

- **Bedroom** – Cosmetics, colognes, hair spray, medications, cigarettes, mothballs

- **Bathroom** – Medicines, nail polish/nail polish remover, aerosol sprays, toilet cleaner, disinfectants, air fresheners, glass cleaner, abrasive cleanser

- **Laundry room** – Laundry detergent, bleach, spot/stain remover, pine oil, aerosol sprays

- **Kitchen** – Ant killer, metal polish (silver, copper or brass), dishwashing detergent, oven cleaner, drain clog remover

- **Garage** – Antifreeze, windshield cleaner, gasoline, charcoal lighter, termite killer, garden chemicals, fungicides, flea powder

- **Home workshop** – Solder, lead, cadmium, formaldehyde, solvents, paint thinner

✔ Store all toxic/chemical products and medicines out of reach, out of sight, and locked away.

✔ Remember to return items that pose a poison danger to safe storage once you're done using them.

✔ Store poison hazards in their original containers.

✔ Never store poison hazards in food or beverage containers.

✔ Supervise your child whenever you use a toxic product with him in the vicinity; and never leave the product out and unattended.

✔ Take proper precautions with medications:

- Make sure all medicines and vitamins are in child-resistant containers

- Always store medications in the original containers with the original labels

- Dispose of any expired medicines

✔ Make sure you have no poisonous house plants in your home.

✔ What should you do in the event of an accidental poisoning?

- If your child is in immediate distress, call 911

- If your child is alert, call the National Poison Control Center at **1-800-222-1222**

This completes our overview of poison hazards. Next, let's turn to the common water hazards that can endanger infants and toddlers in the home.

CHAPTER

12

Water Hazards

Water is like a magnet for young children, who are drawn to it from the time they first notice it's not at all like solid things. They want to play in or near it. They want to experiment with it. They won't leave it alone, pretty much. And even when they're skittish about it, they find water fascinating.

As a safety matter, the bottom line on water is this: It poses a very real danger to young children, especially those under 5 years of age. The danger is drowning, which is the second leading cause of accidental death among this age group, after motor vehicle accidents. We hear about a child drowning and generally picture an accident in a pool or at a lake – something deep and obviously hazardous. But infants and toddlers can drown in water as shallow as 2 inches. As it happens, children this young are most likely to drown at home, in standing water *other than a pool*. In bathtubs, spas, buckets, and toilets, in other words. Every month in the United States, approximately 10 children drown in these water hazards.

The deadly threat water poses obligates parents with young children to be extra attentive to water safety in their homes. The first word in water safety is prevention. And prevention involves 3 key things:

- Blocking children's access to water hazards (e.g., installing a safety clip on a toilet).

- Removing hazards (e.g., draining the bath water as soon as a baby's bath is done).

- Supervision – Nothing beats attentive supervision as a key to avoiding accidental drowning. If you're watching your infant or toddler closely, she'll never have the opportunity to come to harm.

Practicing proper safety will ensure that your child's experience with water is accident free.

Our aim in this chapter is to cover safety considerations with the most common water hazards at home: bathtubs, spas, buckets, toilets, and swimming pools. Let's take them one at a time.

BATHTUBS AND BATH TIME

Once your newborn graduates from a sponge bath to an immersion bath, you'll be dealing with bathtub safety issues. An infant or toddler in a drawn bath is the proverbial accident waiting to happen. More children drown in baths than in all other home water hazards combined. And the majority of these bathtub victims haven't reached their first birthday.

Accidental bathtub drownings happen for one reason, really – inadequate supervision. The sacred rule of bathtub safety is to never leave your baby alone or unsupervised. Not even for a moment. Always stay within arm's reach and keep your eye on her at all times. If you choose to leave the area for any reason – to answer the phone, to grab a towel, whatever – pull your child from the tub and take her with you. No solo "dashes" while she stays in the tub.

Many parents put their baby in a bathtub seat or ring for bath time. This device has suction cups on its underside that stick temporarily to the bottom of the tub, immobilizing the seat. A baby is able to sit up in the ring, which holds her in place. These seats are a terrific convenience for mom and dad, whose hands are freed up to scrub and rinse while their infant splashes. But they are no substitute for your constant supervision. A bathtub ring is *not* a safety device. Therefore, you must never rely on it as a drowning safeguard. Putting your baby in a bathtub seat doesn't free you to leave her unattended. Be aware that the suction cups could come loose, causing the seat to tip over, with the baby in it. (For this reason, you really shouldn't use a bath ring in a non-skid or slip-resistant tub because the suction cups won't adhere reliably to the surface.) Also, a baby might slip through the openings between the seat supports and become trapped beneath the water.

When your baby's bath is over, you should take the following precautions:

+ A wet baby is slippery. Thoroughly rinse the soap from your infant before you lift her. And always lift her with one hand beneath her bottom to support her weight.

+ Drain the bath water immediately. An empty tub poses no drowning danger to an infant or toddler who might somehow reach it.

As your baby becomes a toddler, she'll get more adept in the bath. More self-sufficient. And that could lull you into thinking that it's okay to leave her alone in the tub, at least briefly. Not so. No toddler (or preschooler, for that matter) is far enough along to be left unsupervised in a bath. Tragedy can strike so quickly when it comes to standing water. Our sacred rule about bath safety applies as much with toddlers as with babies.

Now, suppose you have an elder child who's preschool age or a little older. And say your older one, who's responsible for her age, volunteers to watch her baby sibling in the tub while you step out of the bathroom to tend to something. Do you let her? No – absolutely not. An older sibling, mature as she might seem to be, should not be entrusted with this responsibility. Not even briefly.

Safety Note

Bathtub Seats

According to the American Academy of Pediatrics (AAP), use of bathtub seats may actually increase the risk of drowning by increasing the likelihood that babies will be left alone in the tub. Often, parents come to think that it's safe to leave their infant alone in a bath ring. They mistakenly consider the seat to be a safety device, which it is not.

Never leave your infant alone or unsupervised in a bath ring. Make this an ironclad rule.

►BUCKETS◄

Did you know that buckets are the second leading cause of in-home drownings among young children? Most of these happen in 5-gallon buckets used for mopping floors and other household cleaning. A 5-gallon bucket with as little as an inch of water in it poses a serious drowning hazard to infants and toddlers. Most drowning victims are between 8 and 12 months old. What typically happens is an unsupervised baby uses the bucket to pull herself to a standing position, leans forward to reach the water inside, and falls in head first. The bucket's tall, straight sides and weight (the weight of the water plus the baby's weight) then make it impossible for the top-heavy infant to escape. She's trapped, face first in the water.

About 15"

5-Gallon Container

A bucket with a mop is a ripe target for a curious infant or tot. To prevent a tragic accident in your home, never leave your baby unsupervised around a 5-gallon bucket that contains any water or liquid cleanser. When you're through using the bucket, be sure to empty the contents immediately.

►SPAS, HOT TUBS, & WHIRLPOOLS◄

Children under 5 years of age drown in spas, hot tubs, and whirlpools almost as frequently as they do in buckets. (Spas, hot tubs, and whirlpools are the same in terms of the drowning danger. Therefore, we will use "spa" hereafter to refer to all three.) Such deadly accidents typically happen when an unsupervised infant or toddler gains access to a spa and falls in. How is it that the child reaches the hazard? Through a gate or sliding door that was left open or unlocked.

If you have a home spa, take the following precautions:

+ Never allow your child near it unless you or another adult is supervising her closely.

+ Access to it should be blocked by a door or gate with a functioning lock. Make sure this barrier is always closed and locked when the spa is not in use.

+ As a further barrier to entry, you should put a safety cover over the spa when it's not in use. This cover should be lockable.

Be careful when selecting a safety cover. A child can slip beneath some soft covers (solar ones, for example) without displacing them. Thus, parents might not even realize their child had entered the water beneath such a cover because it would appear to still be in place.

TOILETS

Did you ever suspect that your toilet was a drowning danger? The fact is that an older infant or toddler can drown in the shallow water of a toilet. (A falling toilet seat lid is another hazard to be aware of. A falling lid is heavy enough to cause injury if it lands on a baby's head or neck.) This typically happens in the same manner as accidental bucket drownings. The child falls in head first and gets trapped face down in the water.

With toilets, preventing an accident is a matter of denying your child access. It starts – you guessed it – with attentive supervision. Know where she is. Don't let her wander off toward the bathroom alone. Also, get in the habit of pulling bathroom doors shut tight so a little person can't gain entry. Keep toilet seat lids lowered, as a rule. And consider installing toilet clips or locks, which prevent little hands from lifting up toilet seats.

SWIMMING POOLS

Every year, on average, 250 children under 5 years of age drown in pools. The risk of this happening increases once a baby begins crawling at around 9 months old. This is the threshold age at which a child is becoming mobile enough to get to a backyard pool under her own powers. (Don't ever underestimate a baby's range of maneuver on all fours!)

Pool drownings involving young children happen quickly, silently, and without warning. What typically occurs is this: A toddler escapes from her house undetected by a parent, or slips away from a parent while outside, then finds her way to the pool and falls in. Of course, such an accident could never happen without 2 factors being at play: 1) a momentary lapse in or lax adult supervision; and 2) inadequate barriers to pool entry.

Drowning prevention begins with alert supervision of your infant or toddler. If you're a pool owner, you have to keep close tabs on where your child is at all times. And you must never leave her unattended anywhere in the vicinity of the pool.

Barriers to Entry

Beyond supervision, you must install adequate barriers to entry around your pool. As a pool owner, you're probably required by local law to have a perimeter fence around your yard or pool area. This fence serves, foremost, to keep any uninvited outsiders – children from the neighborhood, most likely – from accessing the pool.

Your perimeter fence deters "pool hoppers" and affords you some privacy. It does not, however, provide sufficient protection against opportunistic pool entry by an older infant or toddler. What you also need, therefore, is a child-resistant pool barrier, which is the single-most effective device for preventing accidental drowning of children under

the age of 5 years. This barrier should be installed completely around the pool, about a foot from the pool's edge. A child-resistant pool barrier ensures that an infant or tot in an unsupervised moment won't reach the water's edge and fall in. Such a barrier should be at least 4 feet high and anchored on posts driven into the cement 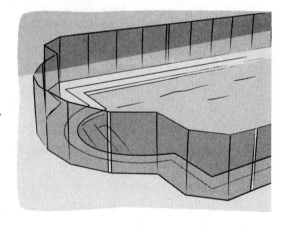 around your pool. Conveniently, it can be easily removed once your child learns how to swim. Make sure its access panels are always locked when the pool's not in use or after you've cleaned the pool. And keep any furniture that could be used to scale the barrier well away from it.

The Consumer Product Safety Commission (CPSC) recommends the following additional precautions to all pool owners with young children:

+ If your house is adjacent to the pool (i.e., if your house forms the barrier on one side of the pool), you should install alarms on any doors that lead directly from the house to the pool area. When activated, these alarms will sound if a door is opened.

+ Also consider installing a pool alarm system, for extra protection. Look for one that meets the American Society for Testing Materials (ASTM) standard. Your best option is to get a system with remote receivers so the alarm is audible inside your house or in other locations well away from the pool area.

+ Don't leave pool toys and floats in or around the pool. These colorful items are likely to draw young children to the water.

+ Consider investing in a power safety cover for your pool. This is a motor-powered barrier that can be easily placed over the water when the pool's not in use.

+ If you have an above-ground pool, always remove or otherwise secure the steps or ladders when the pool's not in use.

The cornerstone of pool safety is prevention. Take all necessary precautions to make sure nothing bad happens in the first place. But prudence says that you should be ready to respond in the event of an accident. Therefore, it's wise to keep rescue equipment by the pool and always have a phone nearby so you can quickly call for emergency assistance. Also, knowing cardiopulmonary resuscitation (CPR) can be a life saver.

We should make one other point: If a young child suddenly goes missing, always look in the pool first. Every second counts dearly when an older infant or toddler falls into a pool. Quick detection and recovery is essential to saving a child's life or sparing her from permanent disability.

Safety Note

Pool Drain Cover Hazard

Entrapment due to powerful suction is a drowning-related danger with pools (and spas, too). Hair or even an extremity (a hand or foot) can get sucked into a drain cover, entrapping the swimmer. This isn't an issue for toddlers, who shouldn't be anywhere near a pool drain cover. But it can be for older children who are novice swimmers. To avoid this hazard, have a qualified pool professional inspect the drain suction fittings and covers on your pool (and spa, if you own one) to make sure they're the right size, attached properly, and up to current safety standards. If your pool (or spa) has only 1 drain outlet, this single outlet might exert tremendous suction force. As protection against this, consider installing a safety vacuum release system, which acts like a "circuit breaker" on the suction force.

REVIEW OF KEY SAFETY POINTS

Let's summarize the key points covered in this chapter:

- ✔ Drowning is the second leading cause of accidental deaths among children under 5 years of age.

- ✔ Children this young are most likely to drown in bathtubs, buckets, spas/hot tubs/whirlpools, or toilets at home.

✔ 3 keys to drowning prevention at home:

- Supervise children closely

- Block their access to water hazards

- Remove water hazards

Bathtubs and Bath Time

✔ Bathtubs are the number one in-home drowning hazard for young children.

✔ Most bathtub drowning victims are under 1 year of age.

✔ Never leave a baby or toddler unattended in the tub and keep an eye on her at all times.

✔ A bathtub seat or ring is not a safety device; never rely on it as a safeguard against drowning.

✔ Never leave a baby alone or unsupervised in a bath seat.

✔ Never let an older sibling supervise your baby in the tub.

Buckets

✔ Buckets are the second leading cause of in-home drowning among young children.

✔ Most drownings happen in 5-gallon buckets used for household cleaning.

✔ Never leave an infant or toddler unattended around a bucket if it contains any water or other liquid.

✔ When you're finished using a bucket, empty it immediately.

Spas, Hot Tubs, & Whirlpools

✔ Never allow your child near a spa, hot tub, or whirlpool unless you're supervising her closely.

✔ Access should be restricted by a door or gate with a working lock.

✔ Placing a safety cover over a spa, hot tub, or whirlpool when it's not in use adds an extra barrier to entry.

Toilets

✔ Keep bathroom doors closed.

✔ Keep toilet seat lids lowered.

✔ Install toilet clips or locks on toilet seat lids.

Swimming Pools

✔ Never allow an infant or toddler near a pool unsupervised.

✔ Install a child-resistant pool barrier around your pool.

✔ Consider installing pool alarms and a safety cover for added security.

✔ Have your pool drain covers inspected by a pool professional (precaution against suction hazard).

✔ If a young child is missing, always look for her in the pool first.

We've finished our overview of water hazards in the home. Let's now turn from drowning prevention to safety considerations with windows.

CHAPTER 13

Window Hazards

Our homes would pretty much be unlivable places without windows. What's a house without them but a fortress? They let in the natural light. It's through them that gentle breezes blow, refreshing our indoors and reminding us of the world beyond our walls. Windows are what we gaze through when we daydream. And how else would we keep discreet tabs on our neighbors if we were windowless?

But regrettably, windows – and window treatments – pose a danger in any home with children under 5 years of age. Accidents involving windows and window coverings injure thousands of young children every year; and tragically, some of these mishaps result in fatalities.

Parents with an infant or toddler need to be aware of the 2 main window-related safety hazards. The first is accidental falls from windows. The second is entanglement in window blind cords, resulting in strangulation. Our aim in this chapter is 2-fold: to describe these main hazards; and to outline precautions you can take to prevent window-related accidents in your home.

➤ WINDOW FALLS ◄

Every year in the United States, thousands of young children come to harm in falls from windows. Those under 5 years of age are the likeliest victims in these accidents, which can be deadly. Over half the injuries and three quarters of the fatalities from window falls involve children who are 3 years of age or younger. And in more than 9 out of 10 cases, falls happen in the victims' own homes.

Falls typically involve the following circumstances:

+ They happen from second- and third-floor windows in single-family homes and apartment buildings.

+ Windows have been left open with only screens in place.

+ They are from bedrooms (the parents' or the child's) or living rooms.

+ Furniture items (sofas, chairs, or beds) are near or under the windows.

Given this pattern of factors, you should take the following precautions in your home to prevent a child from ever falling from a window:

+ Install window guards or window stops in rooms where your child spends time. A *window guard*, which is mounted to the window frame with hardware, has metal bars that prevent a child from falling out.

A *window stop* is a device that prevents a window from opening more than 4 inches – which is the maximum space deemed safe for children. (For this very reason, window guard bars are spaced no more than 4 inches apart.)

+ Open windows from the top whenever possible.

+ Never rely on a window screen as a safety barrier. These screens aren't built to prevent a child from falling out.

+ Don't place furniture close to a window. A bed or sofa near a window is an invitation for a tot to climb up on it to get to the window.

One issue you also should be mindful of is how window guards and stops could affect an emergency fire escape plan from any given room. Every bedroom in your home should have at least one window readily usable for escape in the event of a fire.

WINDOW BLIND CORDS

The cords on window blinds are a lure no small child can resist. Given the opportunity, an infant or toddler will grasp and pull on a dangling cord. Experience warns us that the cord is then prone to wrapping around, or slipping noose-like around, the child's neck, with a potentially deadly result. The strangulation threat is greatest for children under 2 years of age, who are the victims in most fatal window cord accidents.

There are 2 kinds of window blinds: horizontal and vertical. Let's address the safety considerations with each.

Horizontal Blinds

Horizontal blinds, or so-called miniblinds, have an outer cord and an inner cord. The outer cord raises or lowers the blinds, depending on whether it's pulled or released. The inner cord, which is threaded through the slats, does the lifting or lowering when the outer cord is either pulled or released. Both outer and inner cords can pose a strangulation hazard to an infant or toddler. The risk with these cords depends on when the blinds were manufactured.

Outer cords – Window blinds made before 1995 most likely have an outer cord with a closed loop on the end. This loop is the danger

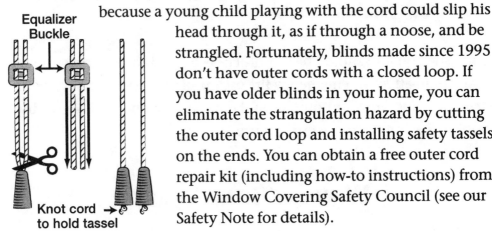

Equalizer Buckle

Knot cord → to hold tassel

because a young child playing with the cord could slip his head through it, as if through a noose, and be strangled. Fortunately, blinds made since 1995 don't have outer cords with a closed loop. If you have older blinds in your home, you can eliminate the strangulation hazard by cutting the outer cord loop and installing safety tassels on the ends. You can obtain a free outer cord repair kit (including how-to instructions) from the Window Covering Safety Council (see our Safety Note for details).

Inner cords – With blinds made before November 2000, the inner cord, when pulled on, can form a loop large enough for a young child's head and neck to fit through. Victims of inner cord strangulation are almost always babies in cribs or playpens situated next to windows. The good news is that window blinds made since November 2000 pose no inner cord danger because of a design safety modification. If you own blinds manufactured before November 2000, you can eliminate the strangulation danger by installing cord stops on the inner cords. Inner cord repair kits are available from the Window Covering Safety Council, free of charge (see our Safety Note for details).

Safety Note

Free Repair Kits for Window Cords

Window blind cords are known to pose a strangulation hazard to an infant or toddler, whose head could slip through a cord loop and get caught. This loop danger is a problem with older window coverings that predate the latest product safety standard for preventing accidental strangulation.

The Window Covering Safety Council (WCSC), which provides consumers with information on window-cord safety, offers window blind owners free retrofit devices for repairing cord hazards on older window treatments. Do you have blinds with cord hazards in your home? If so, you can order a free cord-repair kit from the WCSC, either online (at www.windowcoverings.org) or by or calling the council's toll-free number (800-506-4636).

Vertical Blinds

Vertical blinds have outer cords, which are continuous-loop cords on some models. These cords pose the same strangulation danger as ones on horizontal blinds. If you have vertical blinds in your home, you can eliminate the strangulation hazard by anchoring the cords to the floor or wall with tie-down (or tension) devices. You can get these tie-

Tie-down devices for vertical blinds, continuous loop systems, and drapery cords

down devices for free from the Window Covering Safety Council (see our Safety Note for details).

To avoid the cord hazard altogether, you could install cordless window coverings in your child's bedroom and play areas.

REVIEW OF KEY SAFETY POINTS

Let's summarize the key points covered in this chapter:

✔ Every year, accidents involving windows and window coverings injure thousands of young children, some fatally.

✔ The 2 main safety hazards are falls from windows and strangulation in window blind cords.

Window Falls

✔ Most injuries and fatalities from window falls involve children 3 years of age or younger.

✔ Take the following precautions to prevent window falls:

- Install window guards or window stops in rooms where your child spends time

- Open windows from the top whenever possible

- Never rely on a window screen as a safety barrier

- Don't place furniture near or under windows

Window Blind Cords

✔ Window blind cords pose a strangulation hazard, especially to children under 2 years of age.

✔ Keep cords on all window coverings out of reach of children.

✔ The danger with horizontal blinds depends on when they were manufactured:

- Outer cord hazard on blinds made before 1995

- Inner cord hazard on blinds made before November 2000

✔ You can fix the outer cord on older horizontal blinds by cutting the cord loop and installing safety tassels.

✔ You can fix the inner cord on older horizontal blinds by installing a cord stop.

✔ You can eliminate the cord hazard with vertical blinds or drapery cords by anchoring the cords with tie-down (or tension) devices.

✔ Cord-repair kits for older window blinds are available for free from the Window Covering Safety Council.

This concludes our look at window hazards – which means we've completed our overview of the 4 main hazard categories for young children in the home. It also means we've reached the end of our "guided tour" through the key topics in child safety. Before we go, let's turn our attention briefly to a couple of other topics that parents with a young child (or soon to have a baby) should be considering. Strictly speaking, these don't concern child safety. But they do very much concern your child's welfare now and in an always unpredictable future. They are life insurance and guardian appointment.

CHAPTER

14

Additional Considerations

We've devoted 13 chapters to child safety essentials for parents with young kids and soon-to-be parents. We've identified key safety hazards you should be aware of, and outlined precautions you can take to protect your infant or toddler from them. In all, we have provided a body of information intended to help prevent accidents and the injuries they cause among children under 5 years of age.

In closing, there are a couple of other topics that merit consideration by all parents with young children. They're not directly linked to child safety. But they do bear on the welfare and security of children in a future none of us can predict. Let's introduce them by posing a few sobering questions: What would happen to your child if anything happened to *you*? Would she be adequately provided for financially? Most importantly, who would raise her? These questions bring us to our additional considerations: life insurance and guardian appointment.

⊳ LIFE INSURANCE ◁

When it comes to life insurance, many new and first time parents procrastinate, for reasons not so hard to understand. For starters, life insurance forces us to think about our own mortality. And in the context of parenthood, it compels us to think about the possibility of our children being left behind without us. Then, of course, there's the cost, which can be tough for new parents to afford when they're facing the many other expenses that come with having a child. In some cases, parents adopt the "all or nothing" mentality – i.e., they put off getting any life insurance because they can't afford as much as they want or think they need.

But procrastination doesn't make the issue go away. Something could happen to you and/or your spouse at any time. If it did, you would want your child to be financially secure in your absence. Life insurance is an investment we make as parents to safeguard our children's financial future.

If you don't have life insurance, you should consult with a qualified insurance professional about acquiring affordable coverage that meets your family's needs.

⊳ APPOINTING A GUARDIAN ◁
FOR YOUR CHILD

A guardian is the person who assumes legal responsibility for the care of minor children should their parents die. A guardian generally takes custody of the children and makes all key decisions about their upbringing until they reach legal adulthood. It's your basic right as a parent to appoint who would become your child's guardian. And by law and tradition, you would designate a guardian in a Last Will & Testament.

But say you didn't have a Will at the time of your death. Who would designate your child's guardian (assuming there was no other living parent)? Would it be a brother or sister of yours? No. How about a close friend in whom you confided your first choice as guardian? No again. The decision would be made by the court where your estate is settled. That's who. If there's no Will stating a parent's wishes, guardian appointment is left to the court, which follows state law in determining who becomes guardian.

Given this fact, you can see why it's so important to designate your choice of guardian in a Will. It's your opportunity to state for the record whom you would want to raise your child should anything happen to you. Failure to do so surrenders this decision to the court. And who knows whom the court would choose? It could be someone you never would've considered selecting.

Do you have a Will? If you're like most parents with young children, you probably don't. Statistics tell us that the majority of parents with minor children lack a Will. Let's say you're one of them. And let's suppose, too, that you just don't have the wherewithal to get one done right now. Well, here's good news: there happens to be a quick, convenient, and legally legitimate option available to parents for designating a guardian short of completing a full-fledged Will. It's called a guardian appointment document (or so-called single-purpose Will), and it's only a few mouse clicks away.

Childguardianship.com

You can order a guardian appointment document online through **Childguardianship.com**. This website was created to enable parents without a Will to designate a guardian for their children without further delay. The documents produced through **Childguardianship.com** are as valid as a Will for the purpose of appointing a guardian. A guardian appointment document is a sound alternative until you get around to completing a full-purpose Will, perhaps as part of overall estate planning.

Ordering documents through **Childguardianship.com** is quick (a few simple steps), convenient (ready-to-print documents delivered promptly by email), and inexpensive ($10 or less). Taking this step will give you the comfort of knowing that, ultimately, you will decide who becomes your child's guardian should anything ever happen to you.

APPENDIX A

Summary of Key Safety Points

Here are the key safety points we covered, listed by chapter, for your quick reference.

Chapter 2 *Childproofing*

- ✔ Childproofing covers all the measures we take to protect young children from safety hazards in their everyday environment.

- ✔ Childproofing is no substitute for proper adult supervision.

- ✔ Childproofing is dynamic – as your child grows, you need to modify your childproofing efforts to keep pace.

- ✔ 3 general approaches to childproofing:

    1. Removing hazards

    2. Placing barriers

    3. Cushioning

- ✔ The CPSC recommends the following safety devices for households with children under age 5:

    - Safety latches and locks

    - Safety gates

    - Door knob covers and door locks

- Anti-scald devices

- Smoke detectors

- Window guards

- Safety netting

- Corner/edge bumpers

- Electrical outlet covers and plates

- Carbon monoxide detectors

- Window cord safety tassels

- Door stops and door holders

- Cordless phone

Professional Childproofers

✔ Advantages with professional childproofer:

- Experience (knows the childproofing ropes)

- Expert knowledge of safety devices/equipment

- Access to best safety products

- Works fast

✔ Professionals warn parents to be alert to the following hazards:

- Banister railings (entrapment hazard)

- Toxic cleaners (poison hazard)

- Electrical outlets (electrical shock hazard)

- Salt (can be fatal if swallowed by a baby)

Do It Yourself

✔ 3-step planning for childproofing your home:

   1. Identify all hazards

   2. Specify childproofing steps

   3. Identify safety devices needed to complete childproofing

✔ Solicit childproofing pointers from family members and friends with young children.

✔ Viewing your home literally from your child's perspective (i.e., get down on all fours) may help you identify hazards.

Chapter 3 *The Safe Crib*

Cribs

✔ New cribs must meet all current safety standards; used cribs might not.

✔ The spacing between crib slats should be no wider than 2 3/8 inches.

✔ A crib with loose or missing slats is unsafe for use.

✔ The space between the mattress and crib frame should be no more than 2 fingers wide.

✔ Remove any plastic wrapping from the crib mattress before letting your baby sleep on it.

✔ Never use an adult bed sheet on a crib mattress.

✔ Make sure the crib sheet fits the mattress snugly.

✔ Crib corner posts should be less than 1/16 inch high.

✔ Mattress support hangers should be secured with bolts, screws, or closed hooks.

✔ Never place your baby in a crib with hardware missing or broken hardware.

Bassinets

✔ 3 main dangers associated with bassinets:

- Collapsing

- Tipping over

- Entrapment

✔ Recommended safety features:

- Wide, sturdy base

- Strong, stable legs

- Locking mechanism on folding legs

- Firm, smooth mattress

- Snug-fitting mattress

- Folding hood (on any model with a hood)

- Brake mechanism on any model with wheels

✔ Always place your baby to sleep on his back in the bassinet.

✔ Always lock the wheels in place when your baby's in the bassinet.

✔ Don't permit older siblings or pets near the bassinet when your baby is in it.

✔ Never place a towel or other extra padding on the crib mattress.

✔ Don't put any soft bedding in the bassinet with your baby.

✔ Switch your baby to a crib before he reaches the bassinet's height and weight limits.

Cradles

✔ Be alert to the special hazard posed by a cradle if its locking pins aren't working properly.

✔ Inspect locking pins regularly for damage or displacement.

✔ Make sure your baby's cradle can't rock more than 5 degrees in either direction.

Chapter 4 *Placing Your Baby to Sleep*

Setting Up the Crib

✔ Cover the mattress with a fitted bottom sheet.

✔ Place the crib well out of reach of window blinds or curtains cords.

✔ Don't put any soft or fluffy bedding in the crib.

✔ Don't hang items such as diaper bags or toys on the crib.

✔ Mount mobiles beyond the baby's reach.

✔ Trim any slack from crib bumper ties.

✔ Precautions to follow if tucking your baby in with a blanket:

- Use a thin blanket

- Put baby with her feet near foot of crib

- Pull blanket up no farther than baby's chest and tuck in edges

Putting Baby to Bed

✔ Dress your baby in snug-fitting, flame-resistant sleepwear once she can crawl (around 9 months old).

✔ Always place your baby to sleep on her back.

✔ Do not bring your baby into bed with you to sleep.

Crib Adjustments

✔ Lower the mattress to the middle setting and remove crib toys when your baby reaches 5 months or can push up on her hands and knees.

✔ Adjust the mattress to the lowest setting and remove crib bumper pads when your child can stand up.

✔ It's time to switch your child to a bed when she is approximately 35 inches tall or can scale the side of the crib.

Toddler and Bunk Beds

✔ Toddler beds are great for transitioning from the crib to a full-size bed.

✔ Don't allow a child under age 6 to sleep on the upper bunk of bunk beds.

✔ Make sure bunk beds have secure guardrails on all sides, cross-tie mattress supports, and proper-size mattresses.

✔ Teach children to use only the ladder to climb in or out of the top bunk.

✔ Place a night light in a bedroom with bunk beds so children can see the ladder at night.

Chapter 5 *Guide to Infant Products*

Manufacturer's Instructions

✔ Never ignore the safety warnings on baby products.

✔ Always follow the manufacturer's instructions regarding safe use of infant products.

Used Products

✔ Check the recall status of used products before you purchase them to make sure they're safe.

✔ Be sure to obtain the manufacturer's product instructions for any used product you purchase.

Highchairs

✔ Highchairs should have both waist and crotch restraining straps.

✔ Always strap your baby in the chair with both waist and crotch restraints to prevent him from falling out.

✔ Never use the tray as a restraining device in lieu of the straps.

✔ Take precautions to prevent tip-overs:

- Keep highchair a safe distance from nearest table (so baby can't push off it)

- Keep older children away from chair when baby's in it

Changing Tables

✔ A table without restraining straps is unsafe.

✔ Always use the safety straps to restrain your child when he's on the table.

✔ Anchor the table properly (e.g., to the wall) to prevent tip-overs.

Infant Carriers

✔ The safest infant carrier has a sturdy base, skid-resistant bottom, and waist and crotch restraints.

✔ Always secure your baby in the carrier with the belt restraints.

✔ Never place a carrier on a soft surface (e.g., a sofa or bed) when your baby's still in it.

✔ Never use a freestanding carrier as a car seat.

✔ Never place an infant carrier with your baby in it on an inverted restaurant highchair.

Walkers

✔ The AAP advises against using walkers because they're so unsafe.

✔ Any walker you let your child use should meet the new safety standard established in 1997 to cut down on injuries.

✔ Remove all plastic labels and decals from your walker because they pose a choking hazard to your baby.

Toy Chests

✔ The 2 main hazards with toy chests are a falling lid (causing injuries) and inadequate ventilation (resulting in suffocation).

✔ A toy chest should have the following safety features:

- A hinged lid that stays open in any position

- A lid without exterior latches

- Proper ventilation

Playpens

✔ Slats on wooden playpens should be no more than 2 3/8 inches apart (wider spacing poses an entrapment/strangulation hazard).

✔ On hinged playpens, the collapsible hinges on the top rails should lock automatically when lifted into normal use position.

✔ Never leave an infant in a drop-sided playpen with the side down.

✔ Inspect mesh netting frequently to make sure it's still in safe condition.

✔ Never attach toys or mobiles to a playpen with a string or cord.

✔ Never place your baby in a playpen with a bib, necklace, or pacifier-on-a-string around his neck.

✔ Never put soft bedding in a playpen with your napping baby.

✔ Use only the mattress pad that came with the playpen.

Strollers

✔ A stroller should have the following safety features:

- Brakes on 2 wheels

- A safety belt and buckle that are securely fastened to the seat

✔ Always strap your baby in the stroller with the safety belt and buckle.

✔ Keep your child a safe distance from the stroller whenever opening it or folding it up (to prevent little fingers from getting pinched).

✔ Never place soft, fluffy bedding items in a stroller with your napping baby.

✔ Never use a blanket or pillow as a mattress beneath your napping baby.

Baby Gates

✔ Safety gates enable parents to block a baby's access to hazardous areas and objects.

✔ Old accordion-style gates are very dangerous because their V-shaped and diamond-shaped openings pose a strangulation hazard.

✔ Always use a permanent gate at the top of stairs.

✔ Always install a pressure-mounted gate with the pressure bar on the side away from your baby.

Chapter 6 *Product Recalls*

✔ Every year, children's products of all types get recalled for being hazardous.

✔ Each year, recalled products are responsible for numerous injuries involving young children.

✔ The federal government has a system for identifying and recalling hazardous products that threaten public safety.

✔ Understanding the recall process helps parents to protect their children from product hazards.

✔ Parents must take the initiative in identifying recalled children's products in their home.

✔ Parents must redeem any product recall that affects them (and therefore their child) by following the manufacturer's instructions for repairing or replacing the product.

Chapter 7 *Introduction to Car Seats*

✔ Car seats greatly reduce child fatalities in accidents when installed and used correctly.

✔ Register your child's car seat with the manufacturer so you'll receive notification of any product safety recalls.

✔ A used seat is considered safe as long as it hasn't been involved in a major crash, as defined by the NHTSA. Acquire a used seat only from someone you know and trust to vouch for the seat's acceptable crash history.

✔ Determine the recall status of a second-hand seat before you acquire it.

✔ Avoid purchasing a car seat at a thrift shop, consignment store, garage sale or online auction.

✔ Drive safer by eliminating driver distractions.

✔ Never leave your child unattended in your vehicle.

Chapter 8 *Car Seat Options*

✔ Different car seat types are designed to protect children at different ages/developmental stages.

✔ Car seats are rear facing or forward facing.

Infant-Only Seats

✔ Designed for babies up to approximately 1 year of age.

✔ Children older than 1 year should continue to ride in an infant-only seat so long as they weigh less than the seat's mandated weight limit (20 – 22 pounds).

✔ 2 options:

- Without a base

- With a base

✔ Advantages, with or without a base:

- Convenience of carrier feature

- Smaller seat shell permits better fit (eliminates need for added head support)

✔ Advantages, with a base

- Easy "snap on" installation

- Adjustable base permits proper seat positioning without need for a towel or foam insert

- Most convenient model for placement in middle position in back seat

✔ Disadvantage – A child could outgrow the seat before she turns 1 year old, compelling parents to have to get a convertible seat before her first birthday.

Convertible Seats

✔ Generally for children from birth until they reach 40 pounds (around 4 years old).

✔ Children ride rear facing until they are older than 1 year and have reached the seat's rear-facing weight limit.

✔ Advantages:

- Versatility (rear or forward facing) makes it cost-effective because it's good for 4 years

- Wider harness straps resist twisting and provide more surface area to absorb crash impact forces

✔ Disadvantages:

- Bigger seat shell means a newborn might require added head support

- Lacks the convenient portability of an infant-only seat, which can be used as an infant carrier

Forward-Facing Seats

✔ Designed for children who weigh from 20 to 40 pounds.

✔ 3 harness types available:

1. 5-point harness

2. T-shield harness

3. Tray-shield harness

✔ Advantages:

- Harness strap versatility

- Wider straps resist twisting and provide more surface area to absorb crash impact forces

Booster Seats

✔ Boosts child to height that makes it safe to use vehicle's seat belt to restrain her.

✔ 2 types:

- No-back belt-positioning booster seat

- High-back belt-positioning booster seat

✔ For optimal protection, children should remain in boosters until they're 8 years old or 4 feet 9 inches tall.

High-Back Belt-Positioning Booster Seats

✔ Offers versatility – can serve as either a forward-facing toddler seat or booster seat.

✔ Comes with a 5-point harness, which is used to restrain children when they weigh from 20 to 40 pounds.

✔ The seat is converted to a belt-positioning booster seat once a child reaches 40 pounds (around age 4).

✔ Advantage – An economical choice for parents because it can accommodate children from 1 to 8 years old.

✔ Disadvantages:

- Narrower harness straps

- Arm rests on some models can make it harder to fasten the seat belt in the belt-positioning mode

Recommendations

✔ Rear-facing seat: infant only with base.

✔ Forward-facing seat: convertible.

✔ Sequence of seats:

    1. Infant only with base

    2. Convertible

    3. Belt-positioning booster

Chapter 9 *Car Seat Installation and Use*

✔ Car seats dramatically reduce child fatalities when installed and used correctly.

✔ As many as 4 out of 5 car seats are installed and/or used incorrectly.

Proper Installation

✔ A car seat won't provide full protection unless it's installed correctly and the child is buckled in properly.

✔ The way to be certain your child's car seat is installed correctly is to have a certified car seat technician do it.

✔ Both rear- and forward-facing seats should be put in the vehicle's back seat and, when possible, positioned in the middle.

✔ Never install a rear-facing car seat in the front seat of a vehicle with air bags.

- ✔ 2 systems for car seat installation:

  - Seat belt system

  - LATCH system

- ✔ A properly installed seat shouldn't move more than 1 inch forward or sideways when you push or tug on it.

- ✔ A top tether strap reduces the child injury risk by restricting the car seat's range of movement in a forward crash.

- ✔ Children must ride rear facing until at least 1 year old *and* 20 pounds.

- ✔ It's safest to keep a child in the rear-facing position for as long as possible (i.e., until the child reaches the seat's rear-facing weight limit).

Proper Use

- ✔ Make sure you buckle your child in his seat properly every time.

- ✔ Harness straps should always be positioned at or below your baby's shoulders for as long as he rides rear facing.

- ✔ Harness straps should always be positioned at or above your child's shoulders for all forward-facing seats.

- ✔ Harness straps should be a snug fit against your child – i.e., you should only be able to slip 1 finger beneath the straps at the level of the chest clip.

✔ Proper 5-step buckling sequence:

    1. Place child in the seat

    2. Buckle harness at the crotch

    3. Tighten harness straps

    4. Buckle chest clip at armpit level

    5. Inspect for proper fit

✔ If a car seat shell is too roomy to support a newborn's head properly, fill in the space with extra cushioning (e.g., a small rolled-up towel).

Booster Seats

✔ Always use both the vehicle's lap and shoulder belts to buckle your child in a belt-positioning booster seat.

✔ Never place the shoulder belt behind your child's back or under his arm.

✔ The shoulder belt should cross your child's chest and rest snugly on his shoulder.

✔ The lap belt should rest low across the pelvis or hip area – not across the stomach.

Chapter 10 *Choking Hazards*

✔ Children under age 5 are at higher risk of choking.

✔ Food, toys, and small household items all pose a choking hazard to infants and toddlers.

✔ The choking risk increases when a baby starts crawling and eating table food.

✔ Parents should consider learning basic first aid skills so they can respond immediately if their child is choking.

Meal or Snack Time

✔ Be alert to the following common food choking hazards:

- Hot dogs

- Meat or cheese chunks

- Whole grapes

- Raw vegetables

- Nuts and seeds

- Popcorn

- Peanut butter

- Raisins

✔ Cut food for infants and toddlers into pieces no bigger than 1/2 inch in diameter.

✔ Don't permit your child to eat unless she's sitting down.

✔ Don't let your child walk, run, play, or lie down with food in her mouth.

✔ Always supervise your child during meal or snack time.

✔ Remind your child to eat slowly, take a bite at a time, and chew thoroughly before swallowing.

✔ Don't give your infant or toddler food in the car.

✔ Hard and chewy candy and chewing gum are serious choking hazards for children under age 5.

Play Time

✔ Be alert to the following common nonfood choking hazards:

- Latex balloons

- Small balls

- Marbles

- Toys with small parts

- Toys that can be compressed to fit entirely into a child's mouth

- Coins

- Pen or marker caps

- Small button-type batteries

- Medicine syringes

✔ Never permit your infant or toddler to play with coins.

✔ Keep small household items locked up or dependably out of reach.

✔ Once your baby's crawling, check regularly for possible hazards on floors, under furniture, and between chair and sofa cushions.

✔ Always supervise older children to make sure they don't hand a choking hazard to a baby sibling.

✔ Products marketed for children 3 years of age or younger must meet minimum size requirements to prevent choking:

- Products in general must be greater than 1.25 inches in diameter

- Pacifiers must be greater than 1.68 inches in diameter

- Small balls must be greater than 1.75 inches in diameter

✔ Always heed the manufacturer's recommended age minimum for toys.

✔ Practice balloon safety:

- Don't let children younger than 8 years of age play with un-inflated balloons

- Immediately collect and dispose of broken pieces when a balloon bursts

✔ Don't let your infant or toddler play with a ball unless it's greater than 1 3/4 inches in diameter.

Chapter 11 *Poison Hazards*

✔ The vast majority of accidental poisonings happen in the home and involve such common household items as cleaning products, cosmetics, and medicines.

✔ The majority of unintentional poisonings in the home involve children under 6 years of age.

✔ The accidental poisoning risk rises when babies start to crawl.

✔ Poison prevention involves 2 basic steps: 1) Identify all items in your home that pose a poison risk; and 2) Store these items where your child cannot get to them.

✔ Be alert to common household poison dangers and where they're usually located:

- **Bedroom** – Cosmetics, colognes, hair spray, medications, cigarettes, mothballs

- **Bathroom** – Medicines, nail polish/nail polish remover, aerosol sprays, toilet cleaner, disinfectants, air fresheners, glass cleaner, abrasive cleanser

- **Laundry room** – Laundry detergent, bleach, spot/stain remover, pine oil, aerosol sprays

- **Kitchen** – Ant killer, metal polish (silver, copper or brass), dishwashing detergent, oven cleaner, drain clog remover

- **Garage** – Antifreeze, windshield cleaner, gasoline, charcoal lighter, termite killer, garden chemicals, fungicides, flea powder

- **Home workshop** – Solder, lead, cadmium, formaldehyde, solvents, paint thinner

✔ Store all toxic/chemical products and medicines out of reach, out of sight, and locked away.

✔ Remember to return items that pose a poison danger to safe storage once you're done using them.

✔ Store poison hazards in their original containers.

✔ Never store poison hazards in food or beverage containers.

✔ Supervise your child whenever you use a toxic product with him in the vicinity; and never leave the product out and unattended.

✔ Take proper precautions with medications:

- Make sure all medicines and vitamins are in child-resistant containers

- Always store medications in the original containers with the original labels

- Dispose of any expired medicines

✔ Make sure you have no poisonous house plants in your home.

✔ What should you do in the event of an accidental poisoning?

- If your child is in immediate distress, call 911

- If your child is alert, call the National Poison Control Center at **1-800-222-1222**

Chapter 12 *Water Hazards*

- ✔ Drowning is the second leading cause of accidental deaths among children under 5 years of age.

- ✔ Children this young are most likely to drown in bathtubs, buckets, spas/hot tubs/whirlpools, or toilets at home.

- ✔ 3 keys to drowning prevention at home:

    - Supervise children closely

    - Block their access to water hazards

    - Remove water hazards

Bathtubs and Bath Time

- ✔ Bathtubs are the number one in-home drowning hazard for young children.

- ✔ Most bathtub drowning victims are under 1 year of age.

- ✔ Never leave a baby or toddler unattended in the tub and keep an eye on her at all times.

- ✔ A bathtub seat or ring is not a safety device; never rely on it as a safeguard against drowning.

- ✔ Never leave a baby alone or unsupervised in a bath seat.

- ✔ Never let an older sibling supervise your baby in the tub.

Buckets

- ✔ Buckets are the second leading cause of in-home drowning among young children.

- ✔ Most drownings happen in 5-gallon buckets used for household cleaning.

- ✔ Never leave an infant or toddler unattended around a bucket if it contains any water or other liquid.

- ✔ When you're finished using a bucket, empty it immediately.

Spas, Hot Tubs, & Whirlpools

- ✔ Never allow your child near a spa, hot tub, or whirlpool unless you're supervising her closely.

- ✔ Access should be restricted by a door or gate with a working lock.

- ✔ Placing a safety cover over a spa, hot tub, or whirlpool when it's not in use adds an extra barrier to entry.

Toilets

- ✔ Keep bathroom doors closed.

- ✔ Keep toilet seat lids lowered.

- ✔ Install toilet clips or locks on toilet seat lids.

Swimming Pools

- ✔ Never allow an infant or toddler near a pool unsupervised.

- ✔ Install a child-resistant pool barrier around your pool.

✔ Consider installing pool alarms and a safety cover for added security.

✔ Have your pool drain covers inspected by a pool professional (precaution against suction hazard).

✔ If a young child is missing, always look for her in the pool first.

Chapter 13 *Window Hazards*

✔ Every year, accidents involving windows and window coverings injure thousands of young children, some fatally.

✔ The 2 main safety hazards are falls from windows and strangulation in window blind cords.

Window Falls

✔ Most injuries and fatalities from window falls involve children 3 years of age or younger.

✔ Take the following precautions to prevent window falls:

   - Install window guards or window stops in rooms where your child spends time

   - Open windows from the top whenever possible

   - Never rely on a window screen as a safety barrier

   - Don't place furniture near or under windows

Window Blind Cords

✔ Window blind cords pose a strangulation hazard, especially to children under 2 years of age.

✔ Keep cords on all window coverings out of reach of children.

✔ The danger with horizontal blinds depends on when they were manufactured:

   - Outer cord hazard on blinds made before 1995

   - Inner cord hazard on blinds made before November 2000

✔ You can fix the outer cord on older horizontal blinds by cutting the cord loop and installing safety tassels.

✔ You can fix the inner cord on older horizontal blinds by installing a cord stop.

✔ You can eliminate the cord hazard with vertical blinds or drapery cords by anchoring the cords with tie-down (or tension) devices.

✔ Cord-repair kits for older window blinds are available for free from the Window Covering Safety Council.

APPENDIX B

Child Product Inventory Form

We developed this form as a tool for parents to keep an inventory of their children's products. This inventory will come in handy when you're trying to determine if a product you own is subject to a safety recall. When you're ready to begin inventorying, you can either photocopy the form or print out a version of it from our website at **www.thechildsafetyguide.com**.

Product Type: *Crib*

Manufacturer   _____

Make/Model Number   _____

Date/Place Purchased   _____

Product Type: *Highchair*

Manufacturer   _____

Make/Model Number   _____

Date/Place Purchased   _____

Product Type: *Stroller*

Manufacturer   _____

Make/Model Number   _____

Date/Place Purchased   _____

Product Type: *Playpen*

Manufacturer   _____

Make/Model Number   _____

Date/Place Purchased   _____

Product Type: *Carrier*

Manufacturer   _____

Make/Model Number   _____

Date/Place Purchased   _____

Product Type: *Swing*

Manufacturer   _____

Make/Model Number   _____

Date/Place Purchased   _____

Product Type: *Activity Center/Entertainer*

Manufacturer   _____

Make/Model Number   _____

Date/Place Purchased _____

Product Type: _____

Manufacturer   _____

Make/Model Number   _____

Date/Place Purchased _____

Product Type: _____

Manufacturer   _____

Make/Model Number   _____

Date/Place Purchased _____

Product Type: _____

Manufacturer   _____

Make/Model Number   _____

Date/Place Purchased _____

Car Seat Log

We developed this log as a tool that enables parents to have essential information about their car seat(s) at their finger tips. This information will help you determine when your child has outgrown his or her seat. It also will come in handy if you need to check the recall status of a seat. When you're ready to fill out the log, you can either photocopy it or print out a version of it from our website at **www.thechildsafetyguide.com**.

Seat #1

Car Seat Manufacturer   _____

Make/Model Number   _____

Manufacturing Date   _____

Rear-Facing Weight Limit   _____

Forward-Facing Limit   _____

Seat Type: ❑ Infant Only   ❑ Convertible
              ❑ Forward Facing   ❑ Booster

Seat #2

Car Seat Manufacturer _____

Make/Model Number _____

Manufacturing Date _____

Rear-Facing Weight Limit _____

Forward-Facing Limit _____

Seat Type: ❑ Infant Only ❑ Convertible

  ❑ Forward Facing ❑ Booster

Seat #3

Car Seat Manufacturer _____

Make/Model Number _____

Manufacturing Date _____

Rear-Facing Weight Limit _____

Forward-Facing Limit _____

Seat Type: ❑ Infant Only ❑ Convertible

  ❑ Forward Facing ❑ Booster

Seat #4

Car Seat Manufacturer   _____

Make/Model Number   _____

Manufacturing Date   _____

Rear-Facing Weight Limit   _____

Forward-Facing Limit   _____

Seat Type: ❑ Infant Only   ❑ Convertible
             ❑ Forward Facing   ❑ Booster

Seat #5

Car Seat Manufacturer   _____

Make/Model Number   _____

Manufacturing Date   _____

Rear-Facing Weight Limit   _____

Forward-Facing Limit   _____

Seat Type: ❑ Infant Only   ❑ Convertible
             ❑ Forward Facing   ❑ Booster

APPENDIX D

Online Resources through www.thechildsafetyguide.com

Throughout the book, we've referred readers to this appendix for guidance on locating various child safety resources online. Our clearinghouse for these resources is the companion website to *The Child Safety Guide for New and Expecting Parents*: **www.thechildsafetyguide.com**.

We developed **thechildsafetyguide.com** with reader convenience in mind. The site is your online "portal" to the full range of child safety resources to which we've referred. Thus, it's the only link you need to remember in order to access information supplementary to the book. There's also a practical reason for the site: website links are prone to changing. So rather than print online links that could become obsolete at any point, we've made them available through our website, where they can be updated in the event of any changes.

Please note that there are print-ready versions of our Child Product Inventory Form (Appendix B) and Car Seat Log (Appendix C) available at the site for your convenience.

The online resources available through **thechildsafetyguide.com** include the following :

Databases

+ Car seat technician and installer lists

+ Car seat "Ease of Use" ratings

+ Consumer product and car seat recalls

Forms and Information

- ✦ Car seat registration form (NHTSA)
- ✦ CPSC recall announcements email sign up
- ✦ Child Product Inventory Form (Appendix B)
- ✦ Car Seat Log (Appendix C)

Instructional/Informational Video Clips

- ✦ Car seat installation
- ✦ Child drowning safety
- ✦ Window blind and covering safety
- ✦ Window safety
- ✦ Sleeping safety
- ✦ SIDS reduction
- ✦ Infant products safety
- ✦ Playpen safety
- ✦ Hidden home hazards
- ✦ Poison prevention

thechildsafetyguide.com

 INDEX

About the Author

Christian J. Bezick is the founder and president of the American Family Safety Network, a company dedicated to child safety education, research and resources. He brings to this enterprise a varied and successful business background and his own experience with child safety as a father. Bezick graduated from the US Military Academy at West Point and received an MBA from Northwestern University's Kellogg Graduate School of Management. He lives in Florida with his wife and two sons. When he's not working on child safety, he can often be found at the ice rink playing hockey with his boys.